An Exploration C
Volume 1: Principles & Practice

By
Tammy Parlour

Drawing on the wisdom of Grandmaster Gedo Chang, British Instructor Tammy Parlour reflects on the principles and practice of Ki Meditation. Citing personal experience, she illustrates the modern day applicability of this ancient Korean system. This is a practical guide to Ki Meditation training.

Luke,

You are a wonderful Hapkido Student.

I will miss you.

Sabumnim
(Tammy Parlor)

ACKNOWLEDGEMENTS

Thank you Richard, for being a great 'Ki model'.

Thank you to my parents who drove me to Chang's Hapkido Academy through the Chicago snow before I could drive myself; and for attending each and every one of my Hapkido testing's…from my teenage years through to middle age.

A huge thanks to my partner Jo for reading and re-reading various incarnations of these pages; and for the love and support that made this possible.

And the final thanks must go to my teacher, Grandmaster Gedo Chang, who has inspired me for the past 27years. This book would not be possible without him.

ISBN: 978-1-4477-8121-9

Copywright © Tammy Parlour 2010

www.Ki-Meditation.com
www.ChangsHapkido.net

About the Author

Tammy Parlour began studying Ki Meditation and the Korean martial art of Hapkido under Grandmaster Gedo Chang in 1983 at the age of 12. With 27 years of experience, she is now Chief Instructor for the United Kingdom.

Since moving to the UK from America, Tammy has established Ki meditation schools in the north of England and London. She now runs the London School full-time delivering daytime and evening classes throughout the week, as well as seminars and private sessions.

She has been published in some of UK's leading Martial Arts magazines including *Taekwondo & Korean Martial Arts Magazine* and *Combat Magazine,* and has featured in *Martial Arts Illustrated and Kindred Spirit Magazine.*

Tammy Parlour was interviewed by Hong Kong Legends for their re-mastering of the classic movie *Lady Kung Fu* (AKA *Hapkido*) and features as one of their DVD Extras. She is also the subject of a Martial arts documentary, *Learning from the Masters*, yet to be released.

Preface

The written word is only ever a moment in time. That is exactly how I see this book. It represents over two decades of study, but every day I feel like I am learning more and could write a new chapter. I therefore debated whether to publish such a book – would it quickly become obsolete? I decided by titling it 'volume 1', I allowed myself scope to continue to grow and develop, whilst also sharing the insights and ideas I have now.

I am always reminded of something Master Chang said to me about 5 years ago. He asked me if I sometimes gave lectures during classes. When I responded that I did, he was pleased, "we lecture to remind ourselves." So this book is my memory.

Tammy Parlour
28 Jan 2010

CONTENTS

Acknowledgements	3
About the Author	5
Preface	7
Introduction	13
SECTION ONE – THEORY	**17**
Ki as unlimited potential	19
Why Ki Meditation?	25
Seven Guiding Concepts	33
1. Where the mind goes; Ki flows.	35
2. Energy keeps flowing.	38
3. Our mind leads our body.	41
4. We are today what we did repeatedly.	44
5. Letting Go.	46
6. Our Ki is our responsibility.	51
7. Lighten Up.	54
SECTION TWO – PRACTICE	**57**
Preparation	59
Exploring Breath	65
Exploring the Tan Jon	73
Experiencing Movement	77
Standing Position	83
Kneeling Position	93
Lying Position (Face Down)	97
Sitting Position	101
Lying Position (Face Up)	105
Experiencing Sitting	111
SECTION THREE – MYTHS, LEGENDS & STORIES	**121**
The Tea Master	123
The Best Warrior	124

The Moula teaches his disciples	125
Won Hyo	125
Kyong Ho	126
The Cockerel Fight	127
The Monk who can be cut into ten pieces	128
Being the best Karateka	128
The beautiful flower	129

SECTION FOUR - APPENDICES — **131**
    Appendix 1 – Glossary — 133
    Appendix 2 - Specialised Breathing Techniques — 137

Afterward — 143
Works Cited — **147**

INTRODUCTION

Breathing and meditation methods have become increasingly popular over the past decade. As the pace and the demanding nature of our lifestyles increase, many are looking for a spiritual and emotional pursuit to bring a sense of balance back to their stressed modern existence. Indian Yoga, Chinese Chi Gong and Japanese Zen all have become part of our contemporary vocabulary, yet the Korean philosophical arts have been largely absent from view.

The roots of Korean Ki Training
First suppressed by the Confucian movement in the 12th century, and more recently in the early 20th century during Japanese occupation, the Korean arts would have disappeared entirely had it not been for a few dedicated masters who took to the mountains and hid from persecution. Many were Buddhist monks who continued the practice in secret until the end of Japanese occupation in 1945. Thanks to the dedication of such masters and the preservation of their knowledge, the ancient Korean philosophical arts are finally filtering out and being taught openly.

My reason for writing this book is to introduce others to the training and teachings of my instructor, Grandmaster Gedo Chang. For centuries, Ki theory and practice has been passed down from teacher to student. I hope that through me this process can continue, and that these words and this practice will go on to inspire and enlighten for years to come.

Knowledge of theory without practical study will lack the depth of insight that is possible. This book therefore, represents a basic exploration which will hopefully inspire the reader to further his own understanding through practical study.

Grandmaster Gedo Chang

The son of a monk, my instructor Gedo Chang, grew up in a Buddhist mountain monastery in Chungnam province, South Korea. He lived in these remote hills until his early twenties, learning Ki and the Martial Arts from his father.

Gedo Chang studied religion and psychology at university and became formally recognised as a master of Hapkido in 1964. He opened a Hapkido school in Korea and called it "Wol Ge Kwan" which means "The Victor's Laurel". Master Chang also trained the Korean police forces and was awarded *Best Martial Arts Instructor* by the Korean government.

Finally, Gedo Chang moved to America in 1971 and set up a Ki Meditation and martial arts school in the Chicago suburbs, Chang's Hapkido Academy.

Today, Master Chang continues to teach and lecture across America and Europe. For the past twenty-seven years I have witnessed him inspire people through his lectures. There is something that one experiences in his presence that goes beyond the words he speaks and makes it to the core of who we are. Perhaps this is one meaning of Ki?

As Master Chang himself says, "The true centre of Master actually comes from his personality; an ability to love people and influence them in a more positive direction." He says that the real meaning of 'Ki' can not be read about or written down. It emerges out of you, from the inside.

Despite the inherent flaws in trying to write this text, I think there are profound lessons to be learnt from his teachings. I will attempt to translate the sophisticated concepts of Ki Meditation into an accessible format that is relevant to daily life.

Section one will focus on the philosophical ideas that underpin Ki Meditation practice. I will first introduce the reader to the reasons students practice Ki meditation and the psychological benefits that can be achieved. I will then attempt to discuss some of Master Chang's key philosophical concepts and the basic beliefs central to Ki Meditation training.

It is impossible to fully separate the philosophy from the practice, but section two will look at Ki training from a more practical perspective. This is not a technical manual, but I will share some basic breathing exercises and postures. I will also discuss the physical benefits that can come through the practice of Ki Meditation.

Finally, the third section contains some of the teaching stories used by Master Chang and myself. The purpose of such stories is to inspire questions and insights which will help the student open their minds and gain new perspectives. In a later book I hope to explore the link between Ki meditation and human relationships in more depth.

하나
hana / (1) one

THEORY

KI AS UNLIMITED POTENTIAL

When writing this book I did everything possible to avoid including this chapter. When finally I came to terms with the fact that a book on Ki Meditation couldn't avoid saying something on Ki, I started writing, and re-writing, and re-writing. Nothing I wrote seemed to come close to defining or pinpointing the real essence of Ki. You see, I don't think of Ki as an intellectual concept; so everything I wrote seemed academic and convoluted.

But maybe that's the point? The true essence of Ki, as an intellectual concept, is indefinable. We can talk about its' qualities; we can talk about how being 'full of Ki' feels. But to nail it down and say 'this is it', and do it justice, is an impossible task.

Lao Tzu wrote in Chapter one of the Tao Te Ching.
> *The Tao that can be told is not the eternal Tao.*
> *The name that can be named is not the eternal name*

And so, if we believe the Chinese philosopher, I start an unattainable task. To the student trying to grasp some level of understanding, however, my musings may provide some help.

In the Korean language the ideogram for Ki is used in conjunction with many other words, for example, Ki-gae (self-respect), Ki-ryuk (vigour), Sang-ki (vigorous and happy animation), Ki-seung (strong mindedness) and In-Ki (control or influence over others). Perhaps by understanding other words that use Ki we might further our understanding of Ki itself.

Hapkido students will be most familiar with the term Ki-hap. Ki-hap is the name of the shout that a martial artist yells when executing a technique. The Ki-hap, though on the surface a simple noise, is actually a concentration of spirit, and significantly adds to the power of the technique by stimulating the body and focusing the mind.

Another term Master Chang often speaks of is Ki-Boon. Ki-boon refers to a partial portion of our Ki; it is a psycho emotional reaction (a feeling or state of mind), and a state of feeling at a particular time (our mood). When you have good Ki-boon you are less likely to get sick; you are more positive and more constructive. Bad Ki-boon leads to destructive, negative, judgemental, less forgiving and more cynical thoughts and feelings. As our subconscious mind cannot distinguish between reality and imagination, our feelings and beliefs are incredibly important. Any meaningful activity has a decent chance of brightening your mood, but Master Chang advises

10 Tips for Good Ki Boon:
1. *Work hard*
2. *Play hard (re-creation)*
3. *Be good always: do unto others*
4. *Have faith*
5. *Enjoy the given circumstances (here & now)*
6. *Make others happy*
7. *Have good friends*
8. *Inform others of good things to come*
9. *Have an orderly life*
10. *Fake it until you make it*

All these different uses of the ideogram for Ki seem to revolve around a type of attitude or a particular frame of mind. A further concept that Master Chang also refers repeatedly to when discussing Ki, is that of mushin.

The literal translation of mushin is "no mind". It is a state of being fully alive, an ongoing expression of pure human nature. When meditating, for instance, 'no mind' doesn't mean that I don't hear a sudden gun shot or the clanging of a bell; I am aware of what is going on, but am not being influenced by it. If we use a more western vocabulary we might say that mushim is 'mindfulness'. As Master Chang himself wrote:

> *Mushim is not the turbulent mind*
> *but the tranquil mind*
> *the empty mind without fear*
> *the natural mind standing aloof*
> *from the secular world*

It is the mind breaking into a smile
in the hear and now
In truth, Mushim is the mind far before
any calculation of the above

The truly great martial artist goes beyond impressive physical moves, moving into the realm where action is unconscious – Mushim.

The notion of Ki, then, can be interpreted in an infinite number of ways, and can have an infinite number of qualities. In simple terms we can say that Ki means 'life force', inner power or inner potential. It is an energy that fills our universe and is constantly in a state of creating. It has no beginning and no ending, but is everlasting existence. As Lao Tzu continues in Chapter 4 to say, *The Tao is an empty vessel; it is used, but never filled.*

This same Ki energy that fills the universe is also present within us. Master Chang teaches that Ki is an unlimited power, but becomes limited within because we worry, have fear, become greedy, feel anxiety, etc. He calls these states 'impurities', and believes that when such impurities are present, our internal energy, our Ki, will be locked up inside. "When we understand how to take care of these impurities within", he says, "Our Ki will automatically be manifested." Master Chang clearly views Ki not as a mystical power that only some possess, but rather the essence of the entire universe and an energy we all hold.

Ki itself is neutral; it is neither a positive nor negative force. Therefore 'strong Ki' doesn't necessarily mean a morally positive or 'good Ki'. Through our intention though, this Ki can be directed in a more positive way. The state of our personal Ki underpins our state of health, both physically and mentally. When our Ki flows fluently in the body it will naturally be manifested as Peace of mind, Power, Wisdom and Love. "Out of all of these", Master Chang would say, "Love is the most important".

WHY KI MEDITATION?

Personal Experiences

In my day-to-day life in London I see people travelling to and from work every day. Many seem to operate in a constant state of hurry. Using the underground, people push in front of me hoping to secure one of the few remaining seats in the carriage. Sighs and other disgruntled noises echo around the car as it enters a tunnel and cuts the signal to a vast array of mobile phones. A slightly grey, smartly dressed gentlemen sitting on my right however is still able to tap away to an urgent email message on his BlackBerry. Diagonally across, a couple of young friends debate something in a glamour magazine. They are speaking in a language I don't understand, but I'm struck by the magazine cover; sparkling advertisements and perfect celebrities are encouraging me to aspire to their latest fantasy diet, again. Our world is getting faster and more invasive; the message is clear we can never do enough, achieve enough, or be good enough.

Despite what the media would have us believe, few people will ever experience a physical assault in their lives. Though they may never be confronted by a physical attack, the majority of people are regularly struck down by fear, stress and anxiety.

Given this hectic backdrop, to some, meditation is seen as an oasis in an increasingly demanding life. It is a small window within a busy week that gives the overworked, overstressed or over stimulated the time to rest, stop the mind and just be. Relaxation is definitely a worthwhile outcome of meditation, but it is just the tip of the iceberg. To those that choose to incorporate meditation regularly into their lives, it can offer a much deeper level of awareness. Meditation is not just a simple relaxation technique as some magazines seem to espouse. Though one might feel relaxed after meditating, it is much more about wakefulness, which means moving beyond simply turning the volume down on our lives but really waking up to our full and unlimited potential. At a fundamental level, meditation is about understanding ourselves, our relationship to others and to the world outside.

Over the years I have noticed or been told of instances big and small that indicate the power Ki Meditation has had to affect people's lives. Recently, for example, I overheard some of my new students comparing notes about how they've begun to change since starting Ki meditation classes. Missed trains and other transport difficulties seemed to dominate their stories, an interesting commentary I thought into London living. What interested me was the degree to which students had noticed a difference in their reactions. Situations that had previously caused anything from mild annoyance to full anxiety or anger were now being approached with patience, understanding and at times even humor.

Another student spoke of going to a convenience store recently and someone staring him down in the street. He said, "The old me would have stared back aggressively wanting to win. But, for some reason I spontaneously smiled and looked away." He told me that as he left the shop he noticed the same guy, now on the other side of the street, in a fight with someone else.

I had a student many years ago, before moving to London, who sought help from me. He was having various physical and emotional difficulties, but one thing I was particularly interested in was his relationship with his flatmate. "She has a hamster," he told me. "It makes so much noise running on its wheel that I can't sleep at night." He said, "My flatmate is purposefully putting it against our adjoining wall to bother me."

I seriously doubted this was the case, but even so I would argue that neither the hamster, nor his flatmate was the problem. It seemed to me that he was giving this small animal too much power over how he felt, and that was something he alone could control.

As silly as it may seem, I suggested that he buy his flatmate a gift for her pet. The act of buying the gift and presenting it to his flatmate changed how he felt about his flatmate, the hamster and indeed the situation. He admitted to me later that the pet was actually quite cute. Giving the gift enabled him to reclaim his power and as such, to change how he felt and how he reacted. In a way, it changed how he was relating to his own mind. A few weeks later I asked him if the hamster was still making noise. "Yes, every night. But, I seem to be able to sleep through the noise now. Actually it's not that loud." He also told me how the relationship with his flatmate was improving.

A student who has been training for over twenty years spoke to me about how regular Ki Meditation practice has allowed him to learn to control his emotions much more easily. He claims that his thinking is clearer and admits to finding himself smiling and just feeling great for no apparent reason. After years of training, he says that he can usually stay calm, relaxed, and clear headed while others are excited or have lost their temper. At work he is even asked to attend meetings they expect could be emotionally charged, as his presence tends to keep others calm and under control.

If one signs up to the belief that how we appear in one area of our life is representative of how we show up elsewhere, then these students seemingly inconsequential experiences actually demonstrate a significant shift in how each is managing their own daily lives – little by little, they are becoming less influenced by circumstances and more in control of their own thoughts, emotions and actions. Such a shift is simply one of many benefits experienced by regular Ki meditators.

The power of the subconscious
Despite the many widely promoted benefits of meditation, people still tell me that they could never meditate because their heads are too busy, they can't stop thinking or that they could never just *think about nothing*. Meditators often use the terminology, "empty your mind". This phrasing is actually not particularly helpful to the beginner, for it sets up a very unrealistic expectation.

There is a part of the human mind which will always be churning out thoughts and ideas. In the early states of Ki training it is extremely unhelpful to think that you will be able to stop that process. On the contrary, Ki meditation teaches a sort of separation. It allows us to recognise a thought, response or situation without getting emotionally triggered by it. Having created a powerful pause within our mental processes we are then able to reconnect with what really matters.

Master Chang often likens the human mind to an iceberg. What you see or are conscious of is a small percentage of the whole. Hidden from view, underneath the water, rests a much more influential power. The subconscious mind is the body of the iceberg, invisible to the naked eye, yet exerting immense influence over that which is more visible.

The subconscious mind exerts influence over every aspect of our being. It regulates hormones in charge of blood pressure, digestion, emotions, libido, pain and arousal. It interprets and records experiences as memory, learns patterns of movement and processes experience during sleep. It prepares us for emergencies whilst also regulating bodily functions, biorhythms and mood. The subconscious mind is working behind the scenes in everything we do.

Master Chang also compares the subconscious to a huge container. As we go through our daily life, he says, we are constantly placing things inside it; our thoughts, prejudices, past experiences and interpretations clutter around in this storage place making us who we are today. Each belief or past experience for example brings with it a degree of potential energy. Most of the time the energy remains in a state of hibernation: barely noticeable, seemingly dormant. Given the right circumstances however, the energy will ignite, flaring up with one purpose, and that purpose will drive our actions.

For example, imagine that you've given up alcohol or chocolate for Lent. Most of the time this is a non-issue, but faced with the right circumstances, a hard week at work or a dinner party with the boss, for example, what seemed so easy to avoid, begins to take on a whole new meaning. Faced with the right circumstances we can become almost robotic in our reactions and can literally find ourselves acting contrary to our original decisions. A snack bar is half devoured even before the realisation that it was bought registers. In other words, what we put into the subconscious from learning and past experience creates the basis from which we act. Our reactions to external stimuli therefore, can be driven by the contents of our subconscious mind.

One problem we face though is that most of us are living without real awareness. We are trapped in dual existence; our mind is one place and our body is somewhere else. How many times have you been driving somewhere, somewhere you go on a regular basis, and you suddenly can't remember passing the last few streets? Or how about reading a book only to realise that you have no idea what the last few pages said because you were thinking about what to have for lunch, or what time to pick the kids up from band practice? Or, as I did earlier today, turn up at a friend's house to the shock of your hosts who had forgotten that they had even invited you?

Ki Meditation aims to teach us to wake up from this life on automatic pilot. Slowly we start to notice ourselves, our own minds. We become more aware of our bodies and the subtle changes that happen within. We become more aware of our thoughts and begin to notice what triggers our emotional states. And the more adept we become at noticing ourselves, the more we can also begin to recognise these states in others.

By recognising and controlling these responses, we can learn to harness the energy of the subconscious in order to maximise our potential as human beings. This is one of the most important meanings of Ki development.

Physical Changes

If we're travelling in a car and get lost, most of us will reach for a map in order to find the way home. The map however is only helpful if we already know where we are. Ki meditation practice firstly brings clarity and an ability to see things for what they really are. In other words it makes us first more aware of our staring point. Through Ki Meditation we begin to get an insight into our own minds. We become attuned to our bodies, become calmer and less prone to anxiety. What could be a more helpful skill?

Research articles and papers are popping up all over the place in support of the belief that psychological state is as key to a healthy body as diet, exercise and external stress. Our body is a reflection of our mind and when the mind truly relaxes at a deep level, the body follows.

During the many years I have studied this area I have witnessed my own body changes and heard countless anecdotes from many students throughout the years. Asthmatic students talk about improving their peak flow measurements, students suffering from stress related migraines report significantly reduced occurrence, and those suffering high blood pressure have brought their blood pressure down to acceptable levels. Female students have also reduced the potency of menstrual cramps and learnt to manage difficulties brought on by hormonal changes linked to the menopause.

Mainstream neuroscientists are starting to take meditation seriously. Research being conducted by the likes of Richard Davidson at the University of Wisconsin, and Dr Sara Lazar at the Massachusetts General Hospital, are demonstrating the plasticity of the human brain and the huge potential meditation has for impacting our neural processes. Science is becoming increasingly interested in meditation, and I look forward to reading much more as the West continues to become more fascinated by the potential and insight offered by the eastern pursuits.

GUIDING CONCEPTS

Over the years I have heard Master Chang speak hundreds of times. His lectures always enlighten the newcomers, but they also continue to inform a long-term student like myself. I may hear the same story for the fiftieth time, but I always listen to it as if it were my first. With this attitude, stories that may have seemed simplistic 10 years ago have revealed an inner depth and deep significance to me. As I have matured, so has each story; they have been faithful friends and offered wise counsel.

More recently I have become aware of seven recurring themes, or guiding concepts, in Master Chang's lectures. The more I understand each, the more I seem to understand myself and how Ki operates within my life. In brief, the concepts are as follows:

1. Where the mind goes; Ki flows.
2. Energy keeps flowing.
3. Our mind leads our body.
4. We are today what we did repeatedly.
5. Letting Go.
6. Our Ki is our responsibility.
7. Lighten Up.

Each concept overlaps and impacts on the others, but I will attempt to discuss them individually. I hope that my reflections will spark some thoughts as to how these guiding concepts manifest in your own life.

1 - WHERE THE MIND GOES - KI FLOWS.

The strength of one's Ki, and our ability to use that energy constructively within our daily lives is directly related to our capacity for positive thought and concentration. Ki Meditation training develops and hones concentration skills and increases attention span. It improves our ability to put attention on any subject and to hold it there for a sustained period of time.

I remember learning to drive aged 15 during one high school summer term. The driving instructor sat in the front passenger seat; I was in the back waiting my turn at the wheel. The girl next to me, also eager for her chance at the controls pointed to a mail box across the other side of the street, "Look at that", she exclaimed. To this day I can't remember what was so special about the mail box, but as we all drew our attention to it, the car followed suit. I remember the instructor screaming "eyes on the road" to the bewildered learner driver as he slammed on his emergency brake pedal and we all lurched forward, a little shell shocked.

In Hapkido terms this same experience can happen when we spend too long worrying about our opponent's size or imagining their kicking ability. Our attention becomes distracted and we get so fixated on something else that we become almost paralysed, controlled by our own fear and imagination. Similarly in the board room we might become so worried about the presence of the CEO that we lose our ability to speak fluently on a subject that we know inside out. By focusing on something we send our energy that direction, diverting it from where we need it to be.

In their study on the effects of stereotypes, psychologists from the University of Exeter and St Andrews University have alleged that "what we think about ourselves – and also what we believe others think about us – determines both how we perform and what we are able to become." (Haslam , 2008) Many scientists assert that how our mind functions and processes the world is more significant than what actually happened. For a few decades sports psychologists have already been exploiting the power of the mind using visualisation. Athletes such as Steve Backley, a former Olympic Javelin Gold Medallist, attribute a big part of their success to visualisation and the ability to mentally rehearse even when injured. The Olympic diver Greg Louganis has also spoken on how visualisation helped him identify what could go wrong when competing, and how to put it right. It seems that what goes on in our heads gets played out in our actions. Imagination becomes reality; what we focus our minds on builds a certain creative energy.

Imagine the sun being shone through a constantly shifting magnifying glass; nothing much will happen other than perhaps a little extra heat. If the same magnifying glass is placed in the sun and held steady, then fire can be created. The magnifying glass doesn't forcefully try to push the rays through its glass; instead it simply aligns itself with nature. In this same way, we do not "create" Ki through using the right tools, instead we learn to concentrate and shift our mental focus thus tapping into our own unlimited supply of Ki energy. When we have total concentration on the here-and-now, we can access this extraordinary potential.

A lot of the time we can find ourselves doing many different things at once. Often while our body is physically in one location, our mind could be in an entirely different place. The usual office lunch is perhaps the easiest example of this. Oblivious to the tastes and textures of our rushed meal, the latest project, anxiety over an upcoming meeting or financial worries become the sandwich fillings of choice. In other words the stressed worker doesn't eat his food, he eats his worries. For a huge percentage of our lives then, our attention is somewhere other than on what we are doing. We lose concentration most when we allow our minds to worry about the future or to dwell on the past. Is it any wonder that we are unable to use the immense power we have at our disposal?

Concentration can be viewed as the 'fascination of mind'. It is effortless and relaxed, not tense and purposeful. The only way to keep the mind in the present is by practice. Every time your mind starts to leak away, the application of Ki Meditation principles can help you to bring it gently back.

2 – ENERGY KEEPS FLOWING.

As I'm writing this it is the start of another year. A week ago on Monday morning, the running machines at the gym where I rent space were packed with eager exercisers. Today, the gym was almost empty; it would seem the idea of getting fit was better in theory.

Actually New Year's resolutions can give us a great impetus to change things in our lives. But to think changing any habit will be a smooth process is a misguided assumption; there will always be obstructions and difficulties that rear their heads as old habits try to regain control.

There is a standard joke with my parents when I visit them in Chicago. They say that they gain a daughter and lose a car. As is the way in most of the U.S., my Mom's car is an automatic. Our car at home in London is manual. Each time I return to drive my mother's car I spend the first few days putting my foot on an imaginary clutch and whacking my left hand into the side of the door as I search for the gear change. Throughout this adjustment period, at no time do I think that I will never be able to adapt or that I'll go home with a broken hand from hitting the door so many times. Each time I bash the door, I remind myself that the car is automatic… again and again… and then suddenly the impulse has gone… until I return to England and must go through the whole process in reverse. When we learn anything new we have to build and maintain the neural pathways. It takes time, but if we persevere we'll get there in the end.

When faced with challenge often a lot of people underestimate their ability to withstand a crisis or difficulty and become too eager to revert to old ways. If you'd asked me if I could have coped with having to leave my family in my early twenties and start afresh in a "foreign" country I would have wondered whether I had the strength. A crisis, be it a challenge to your professional ability, the loss of a loved one, or in my case the loss of security can threaten your sense of identity, it forces you to dig deep and find your real sense of worth. Transition is always uncomfortable at first, but when we keep reconnecting with what is really important in our lives we can withstand so much more than we might have thought possible.

Our mind then flows constantly like water in a stream. It is always working, persistently linking thought to thought, making connections and prompting actions. In the same way that a challenge can unsettle us, a rock placed in the stream will also cause the water flow to change. Just as the water flows continuously by simply adapting its path, so also our thought processes adjust themselves to the changing circumstances adapting to each and every psychological rock.

The CEO entering the room in the middle of your pitch could cause a flurry of emotion and thoughts that divert your attention and energy away from an important presentation. Having the ability to focus on something and see it through to the end without being distracted by our own minds is critical in business, and in our wider lives it is essential for building self-esteem.

Through Ki training then, we gain insight into our own minds; we learn to make the mind a more serviceable tool. We learn to notice the rocks in the stream earlier and earlier, and become more adept at channelling the flow back again and again on to the preferred course. We notice tension patterns and incorrect posture in our bodies; these act as signposts to pent up emotions and learned behaviours. Calming our minds, and becoming more in touch with our own bodies lets us bring the conscious mind back into the present moment.

After an hour's meditation we will be able to hold our flow for a while, but soon we encounter obstacles and the confusion returns – that calm and relaxed focus we had been fostering, gets disturbed again. This skill we are developing becomes easier and easier the more we practice, but it is still a skill that is highly vulnerable to decay. Ki training, therefore, is not a 'once-in-a-while' pursuit, but something that must become a part of daily life if we want to stay proficient at controlling the mind.

How we deal with the inevitable roadblocks we encounter along our path then, or rocks in our stream, will determine what kind of wife, father, employee or Black Belt we will become.

3 - OUR MIND LEADS OUR BODY.

Have you ever watched people in a queue? When the mind is restless or anxious, the feet are rarely still. People will shuffle around from one foot to the other, the more anxious they are, the more they move. There is a direct link between our emotions and our physiology; what we think and how we feel directly effects our physical selves. When habits or posture remain for an extended period of time, they leave their mark on the body.

A quick internet search can unearth a plethora of recent studies supporting this assertion. They claim that exercise can improve mental health, that stress may raise cholesterol in healthy adults, that social isolation and loneliness can impair the immune system and that breast cancer patients who get group therapy live longer. Dr Oakley Ray at Vanderbilt University reported in the *American Psychologist* in 2004 that over 50% of deaths in the US could be attributed to behavioural and social factors (Oakley). Understanding how our mind influences our health and susceptibility to illness then, can bring important changes to our lives. This understanding can help us to better deal with daily stresses and anxieties, whilst offering some protection from illness and the bodily decline brought on by age.

What we are starting to understand as a society, is that physical symptoms of sickness and injury can also have an underlying psychological cause. An example of this could be when pain flairs up predictably in response to a recurring stressful situation. I remember having a Hapkido student for a number of years who always injured himself right before a test. Testing for a new belt is a stressful experience; you are on show, demonstrating your skills in front of your peers and the Master. The mind has a way of shielding us from things we perceive as being too painful; in some situations pain can be perceived as a message of protection from deep within. In this situation, the pain my student experienced gave him an excuse not to test. He remained a white belt (beginner level) for 18 months, something that should have lasted no more than 3 months.

The self reflection encouraged by Ki Meditation practice can help us to resolve these underlying issues. We begin by becoming more aware of the underlying beliefs, fears or anxieties we may be acting out in a given situation. We can accept who we are with compassion, and acknowledge the choices available to us. The clarity developed by Ki Meditation practice enables us to see different ways of achieving a more positive result. In the case of my student, he needed to stop comparing himself to others and separate his worth as a person (self-esteem) from his performance on the mat.

Once we acknowledge the link between mind and body, we are able to achieve so much more. I was reading an article that mentioned Roger Banister recently. On 6th May 1954 in Oxford, Roger Bannister broke the 4 minute mile. Before then no one thought it was physically possible. Amazingly, he didn't have some incredible physical training programme – he trained one hour per day in his lunch break. What seemed to be more important was the mental training he undertook. Before each race he would spend a great deal of time sharpening his running spikes. For him this was a meditation; it was the mental preparation which enabled him to achieve what others could not, breaking the 4 minute mile barrier.

What is possibly more amazing, is that 4 months after Bannister achieved his goal his main rival also went under 4 minutes. Since then 100s have broken the 4min mile. In one moment, Roger Bannister dispelled the belief that it was impossible.

Rightly so, the link between our mental, emotional and physical states is gaining more and more credence. Through Ki Training I have witnessed first hand people gain relief from migraines, insomnia and menstrual discomfort; others have improved their asthma peak flow measurements, reduced their blood pressure and become better at managing pain. Through Ki training we not only still the mind, but in doing so we bring our awareness back to the present moment, this both revitalises the body and allows us to focus our energy and potential right where we need it.

4 - WE ARE TODAY WHAT WE DID REPEATEDLY.

As a martial arts instructor I put my students through lots of repetitive exercises. Through these drills they not only hone their technique but also condition their mind and body in order to react instinctively. When we repeat something enough it becomes second nature; we move an action from conscious control to unconscious control, people often use the expression that "things happen without thinking". This process not only manifests in sport, but in every aspect of our lives.

The famous Taoist philosopher Lao Tzu teaches that *"A violent man will die a violent death"*. In other words the habits we form, both physical and mental, mould us into what we become. In eastern philosophy this is known as Karma: our thoughts, our words and our actions create our future reality.

If our habits create our future reality then helping our children to form good habits must be one of the most important things we can do. With this in mind, the first thing Master Chang teaches young children who attend his martial arts school is to make their beds everyday. He believes that the attitude they develop from such a discipline is invaluable and will spill out into other areas of their lives. "Most accidents," he says, "are actually incidents. We have been programming ourselves in a certain direction and it will find a way to express itself."

In the same way that positive habits can create a more positive future, negative habits will foster a more pessimistic outcome. In order to grow, any seed requires air, water and sun, in other words the right environment. Likewise, if we want positive seeds to grow within us, we must provide them with the right environment. As Aristotle said, "Excellence is not an act, it is a habit".

At some level then, Ki meditation practice is a route to developing good habits within our lives. With this foundation, you become able to handle any positive or negative situation that may confront you; you become a creative force in your own life.

5 - LETTING GO

Shakespeare wrote in Hamlet (Act II, Scene ii), *There is nothing either good or bad but thinking makes it so.*

For the past month, every day on my way to my Hapkido school I have passed a movie poster. I get caught in the rush of people dashing to and from work, so have never had more than a glimpse at the graphics. What I noticed was a woman in a martial arts pose similar to the one taught at Red Belt level in my style. The women was quite old and in period costume so it struck me as kind of strange, but I decided that she was in some sort of horror show and was having to defend her family. This morning I stopped to look at the poster more clearly. What I saw was a woman not in a fighting position of any sort, but resting on a large walking stick. It struck me how easy it is to miss-see something and, to paraphrase many philosophers, that our experience of the world is as we are, and very seldom as it actually is.

On another occasion, in the same train station subway, I heard a loud, piercing alarm. At the moment I touched my travel card to the check point the alarm stopped. For a second or two I wondered if the alarm was related to my turnstile, and thought that perhaps as I passed through I must have fixed it somehow. In hindsight this seems quite an arrogant or narcissistic assumption – that everything somehow must be related to me. As I completed the thought the alarm started again, and to my right I noticed the attendant opening and closing an emergency exit.

We all have particular tendencies. We all view the world through past experiences and mental constructs. Even though our thoughts may be distorted they nevertheless create a powerful illusion of truth. But what we hold up as real or true is often simply just one version of reality.

A friend of mine has been struggling with self-esteem issues for some time; she experienced childhood mental abuse from her father, and bullying at school. When we were first becoming friends she would often misread my emails, at times responding with abusive and argumentative replies. Her habit was to see others as aggressors who would subsequently abandon her. To her, her own aggressive response was not designed to push me away, but was entirely justified; it was a defence mechanism keeping her safe from a wrongly perceived threat. Her own actions almost brought to pass what she feared (being abandoned), so paradoxically in her mind, the world as a scary, lonely place would become more and more true. She was oblivious to how her own mistaken belief and subsequent actions were habits which made it more likely that people would walk away from her.

I read an interesting quote in the Harvard Business Review today which echoes this point. Brain expert John Medina was being interviewed about how understanding neuroscience can impact productivity. He said, *"The brain isn't interested in reality, it's interested in survival. So it will change the perception of reality to stay in the survival mode."* (Medina, 2008)

Once a habit has been created then, or an experience has been deemed as significant by our mind, nothing then feels as safe and as comforting as a repetition of those past experiences. In fact just like in my friend's case, our brains will manipulate reality by creating false feelings and beliefs that further reinforce and perpetuate that habit. Breaking a habit requires that we gain a clearer picture of what we may be acting out in our daily lives; this is an awareness that can be gained through the self reflection that Ki meditation promotes.

This alternative perception of reality is what Master Chang terms 'the false self', a self that we hold on to, but must strive to let go if we want to tap into our full potential. He says that it is what we attach to when we are bound by circumstance or external conditions. Referred to as 'Sam' or 'lachksana', it has charismatic qualities that mesmerize us and divert our attention. The real obstacles then, that prevent us from achieving our full potential are those created by our own minds.

Another friend of mine is a keen squash player, competing avidly in her club's leagues. Typically she and her opponent would play the match and then continue afterwards with some non-competitive games. Up until recently my friend would find time and again that, even against a much less talented player, she would lose the competitive games, only to annihilate the same player in the friendlies. On a similar line, Master Chang talks of the expert archer who hits the target 100% of the time, but when offered £100 per shot will on average miss 40% of the bull's eyes. Perhaps it's the desire to win, perhaps simply the distraction of thinking about something other that what we are doing, but each example demonstrates an individual being influenced by something else. Master Chang would say, "They are no longer one, no longer pure. The mind resides in two places".

In his book The Tao Te Ching, Lao Tzu taught this very thing; he said that we should act in accordance with nature. Our principle problem in life, he implied, seems to be ourselves; we need to get out of our own way. This holding on to what is not real, be it a belief, an expectation or maybe a fear, leads us to being divided and thus unable to use our full potential.

Master Chang goes on to say that as human beings we are spending too much time 'holding'. We become distracted by something that is no longer here. A memory, an emotion or a prejudice become like heavy weights we carry in our pockets. Stuck to the spot, we fixate on them and they stop us from truly growing as individuals. He tells of a story of two monks travelling home after a long retreat. After 2-3 miles the monks stumble upon a fast flowing river that they must traverse in order to continue their journey. A few yards down stands a young women; she also needs to cross the water but is noticeably apprehensive and worried. The first monk rolls up his trousers and wades over successfully. Noticing the women, the second monk picks her up and safely carries her to the other side. The woman thanks the second monk and goes off on her journey in a different direction. After some time, the first monk finally feels he must say something; "How could you touch a woman? We have spent 6 months practising our meditation and in one moment you have broken one of the main rules; you have ruined your training."

The second monk looked quizzically at his companion, "It is you who have ruined your training. You are still carrying her; I put her down a long time ago!"

We become stuck and separated from ourselves when we become influenced by Sam (lachksana, meaning price tag, symbol or sign). We lose our perspective when we become overly influenced by our circumstances, our environment, or when we hold on to unnecessary emotions and beliefs. Being in unity is about the coordination of mind and body. It is about a total concentration on the present moment. When we concentrate in this way, there is "no-self"; we kill distractions and we ignore false beliefs. Through disciplined Ki Meditation practice we get rid of the false self and we let go of this attachment to external conditions that separates us from connecting with our true potential. It is then that our Ki flows full and strong.

6 - OUR KI IS OUR RESPONSIBILITY

Acupuncturists and shiatsu practitioners train to rebalance the energy meridians within the body. Doctors give us medicines to stop the pain or kill the virus. In all these incidences though, if the underlying cause is not dealt with, any intervention is simply a temporary distraction, and the problem will reoccur.

Many of us have become quite proficient at deluding ourselves. I know I have sometimes distracted myself by watching the TV, overeating, over exercising or by convincing myself that actually someone or something else was to blame for my own situation. Through the years, I have found that the more excuses I come up with, the more unfulfilled I have felt. What I am talking about is a victim mentality: the idea that things are beyond our control, so we look around for someone or something else to blame for our lot in life. A victim mentality breeds a sort of spiritual inertia; it is helplessness; it is a reluctance to participate in life. If we face life in this manner we risk getting locked into a cycle that becomes hard to escape. This lack of control we feel in our lives corrodes our self-confidence, affecting us physically, intellectually and emotionally whilst stripping us of any motivational drive. The key to breaking through this response pattern though is taking back responsibility for our own reaction patterns.

I have a student who, one year ago, broke his hand in my Hapkido class. He was practicing kicks, lost his balance and landed wrong. No one pushed or knocked him, he didn't slip off a mat, he just lost his footing and the result was an unfortunate accident. I was so struck by my student's attitude following the injury. Many would have complained about the pain, blamed someone else for it happening, or at least whinged about not being able to fulfil all his responsibilities at work. His response was anything but this. He moved himself off the mat, and quietly asked if he could be excused to go the hospital. As he waited with another student to be seen by the nurse they both laughed together and spoke about work and families. His attitude remained consistent despite later being told by the doctors that he had broken his hand in one of the most painful and unusual ways possible. When asked how he would get from one meeting to another he commented, "Well, I usually drive myself. I will just need to get a taxi for a while". He then added, "Typing will be slower, so I'll get to work a little earlier." He is back training once again, and making great progress.

Really accessing our full potential then, involves taking responsibility for our own lives, our own destiny and changing our behaviour. Change takes time. But if we want to influence things to change positively within our lives we must act; dormancy causes our Ki to become stagnant. It is through our intention that Ki can be directed positively, so we must intend.

I have said that Ki within the universe is a constantly creating energy; Ki within us is no different. When we dare to take responsibility, we are striving to be our full self. We are not striving to be better than another, but we are recognising that we have created who we are, and have the power to re-create that. Freely expressed, Ki is the force within us which moves us to action, gives us initiative, and drives us to overcome the obstacles in our path.

So how do we let our intention manifest itself? We are able to access our full potential only by first letting go of everything else. When our false self has been dropped, and are mind is focused, then we can send our energy direct, fast, and on target.

7 - 'LIGHTEN UP'

At the end of a recent seminar a wry smile crept over Master Chang's face and he said with great delight, "You should practice Ki meditation, but don't be weird". It took everyone by surprise, but as always this light hearted remark held some profound wisdom.

When we are anxious, or fearful, or angry, our minds often get stuck. We might start to obsess over small details or become attached to a way of doing something or to a particular doctrine. "I must always meditate at 6pm, everyday", for instance. Most of the time this discipline can really be useful at helping us develop good habits; but, for example, if you become stressed or unable to change from your normal schedule one day because the plumber didn't arrive on time to fix your washing machine, then I might argue that you are becoming 'weird', and rigid in your actions. Likewise if our behaviour is causing others harm then we must re-examine our actions, perhaps also our belief system and motivations to explore a more harmonious solution.

A state of mind that is rigid and fixed in any situation is a disease. Someone who has mastered himself is someone whose mind is not stuck. Through Ki meditation then, we are creating a mind that resembles fluid water, not ice. Both water and ice have the same composition, but one is rigid and stuck, and the other flows freely.

A mind like water is adaptable, persistent and confident; it is soft, powerful and constantly moving. So as we practice Ki meditation, we are working on melting the ice. When we melt the ice, our whole body becomes free and relaxed. This means we are abandoning anxiety, fear, and prejudice.

Just like having a fixed belief or opinion, keeping our muscles rigid and tense requires great effort; it could be argued that this effort is an activity in itself. When we stop tensing, we are free to use that energy elsewhere. When we 'lighten up' our attitudes our physical tension also releases; stress may reside in the body, but it originates in the mind. So, when we stop needlessly focusing on the past or the future we can fully experience the present.

Master Chang wants us to be in harmony with our environment and approach Ki Meditation with a mind like water. Water remains true to its fundamental nature and persists towards its goal, but it also adapts to its circumstance. By relaxing the mind, we lighten up; we melt the ice.

Conclusion

However hard we may try, practicing Ki Meditation takes time and requires a high level of self-discipline. It requires perseverance and commitment; it is not simply a relaxation technique, but profound self-searching.

Our success depends entirely on our ability to relate appropriately to what is actually occurring in this present moment. Contemplating the seven guiding concepts and understanding how they play out in our own lives brings us closer to uncovering and understanding who we really are.

둘

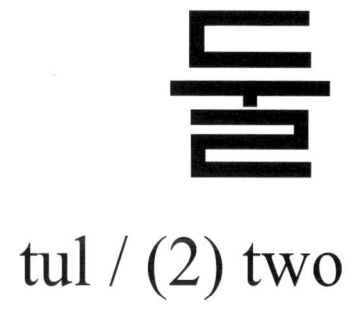

tul / (2) two

PRACTICE

PREPARATION

Whether we practice alone or with others, meditation sessions will differ from one another. On some days concentration will be a trouble free experience; other days you may find challenging and problematic. This is normal for the beginner and intermediate student. The strength and the quality of Ki within us is directly linked to our temperament and mindset. Positive emotions and feelings support and rejuvenate life; we feel balanced, calm, self-aware and more easily show compassion to others. When our energy becomes negative however, we experience blocks and stagnation within our flow of Ki, our well-being declines and disease develops. Whereas the life of monastic piety may not be a viable option for many, Ki Meditation practice can help us better understand and manage those natural ebbs and flows a little easier. Unfortunately many people have either given up or simply believe that they have no control over their given circumstance, allowing their feelings to overwhelm them. Reflecting on the seven guiding concepts, without expecting every session to be perfect will help create the right mental environment for your practice. There are also some practical considerations though that could help make things a little easier for you at the beginning. Creating the right physical environment in which to practice will help you gain the most from the experience. Putting aside regular time, finding a good location and considering your physical state will all influence your meditation.

The right environment

In an ideal world, Ki meditation should be performed somewhere quiet and spacious. Unfortunately this isn't always practical so, provided you have space to move and no obvious distractions, this should be sufficient.

Some of the classes that I teach in London occur right next to a boxing club. The thin wall that separates us does nothing to drown out the repeated pummelling of punch bags or swearing and yelling from the boxers. Beginners may blame the external clatter for not allowing them to concentrate, but life can also be quite noisy. The calmer and quieter we are on the inside the easier it is to cope with external distractions. After a few classes my students find they are able to put our neighbours' noises to one side, and simply concentrate on their breathing.

Regular Practice

After you have found somewhere to practice, the next thing to consider is putting aside regular time. Without regular training the mental skills you are developing will decay over time. Like any skill, meditation must be practiced to be maintained. Reading about meditation is no substitute for actually doing it. Profound understanding and change doesn't come from studying, it comes from practicing; study without practice will always be empty and unfulfilled.

The physical body

Once you have time set aside and found a place to practice, spend time considering your physical preparedness. Overworking, too much sex or exercise or simply not getting enough rest could all become issues; meditation will rejuvenate the body but if the body is too fatigued it needs sleep.

As I often teach a Hapkido class directly after a Ki Meditation session, I find I must eat something before to sustain my energy levels. Moderation in most pursuits is key. Those days that a sugar craving has got the better of me, or I have been taken out for a meal by a student and indulged a little too much, I find my practice is often affected. Consuming a heavy meal or overeating prior to meditation practice is likely to cause concentration difficulties. An empty stomach or light meal is best. Likewise, alcohol, drugs and nicotine all alter brain chemistry. It's best to have a clear relaxed mind when practicing meditation, so if you can avoid these it is definitely preferable. Just remember, what we put into our bodies affects our ability to concentrate.

Support from others

If you have access to a class this is definitely a bonus. Most people find meditating alone quite difficult to stick to; there always seems to be an excuse not to do it. Attending a class gives you access to an expert instructor; it's also amazingly empowering to have the support of a strong and motivated group of people around you. There is something about being in the presence of an agitated mind that makes your mind agitated; conversely being in the presence of other still minds – helps to still your own. Participating in a group may also make it more likely that independent practice will take place between classes.

Superstition

Some forms of meditation encourage other practices such as out of body experiences, or communicating with one's ancestors. But, any emphasis on leaving this world to communicate with another should be actively discouraged. Through Ki Meditation practice we are aiming not to escape the world we are in, but to become fully present and whole in this world.

Occasionally in meditation practice you may experience something out of the ordinary: being able to break boards with your fingertips or seeing an aura perhaps. It's also possible to perform various feats in order to test the strength of our Ki: The 'unbendable arm' and becoming rooted to the ground so others can not lift us are just a couple of these 'tests'. However intriguing these states might be, they are not the purpose of Ki meditation training and we should take care not to become attached to them. To focus too long on them, or to think they are particularly special will cause you to focus on the wrong thing and will lead to stagnation within your practice. If anything like this does occur, see it for what it is and move on.

Conclusion

Reflecting on the state of Ki within ourselves requires that we become more consciously aware of our present circumstances and habits. Our lifestyle (how we exercise, how we eat, what stresses we put ourselves under and what type of environment we create around us) can have a profound effect on our state of Ki. The day to day choices we make all have significant impact on our mental and physical state. Learning to control and understand the mind though, can simply evolve out of the process of controlling breathing.

EXPLORING BREATH

Breathing is one of the few bodily functions that we do both voluntarily and involuntarily. As such, we can consciously use breathing to influence the involuntary or sympathetic nervous system that regulates blood pressure, heart rate, circulation, digestion and many other bodily functions. The most widely used example of this is to take your blood pressure at the start and end of a class; regular students often notice a significant change in their heart rate, something that could be quite useful to anyone suffering from high blood pressure. Breathing exercises therefore, can act as a bridge into those functions of the body over which we generally do not have conscious control.

I was chatting to a student this past week. Previously a stressed city worker who was partial to migraines, he told me how much better he was feeling since starting Ki Meditation training 4 months previously. "I haven't been ill yet!", he declared. "Breathing," he said, "it's so obvious. Why isn't everyone doing it? How come no one told me about it before?"

Everyone breathes. But, as many people get older, lose fitness or become stressed their breathing becomes more and more shallow. Our breathing rate is directly linked to our stress response. Master Chang often says, "We sigh in relief, gasp in pain, and stop breathing momentarily in anger or fright." The faster and more shallow we breathe the higher our level of stress or anxiety. Shallow or chest breathing usually lasts about 2-3 seconds. This, in addition to breathing through the mouth translates as only about 500cc of air being inhaled at a time. As our lung capacity is circa 3500cc one begins to become aware of the huge margin for improvement.

In 1931 Otto Heinrich Warburg won the noble peace prize for his studies of respiration. His key finding was that a lack of oxygen within the body caused disease. When we breathe, air travels in through our nose or mouth, travels down our windpipe and bronchial tubes and enters into the lungs. Oxygen in the inhaled air is transferred by the lungs to the blood and carried to the body tissues. Carbon dioxide, the waste product of this process, is transported back by the blood to the lungs and exhaled. When the body is stressed, the circulatory system closes down the fine capillary network that takes blood into the tissues and our breathing becomes more shallow. The cells may need more oxygen, but there is no way for it to reach them. Oxygen is the fuel which drives many of our bodily processes. If the fine capillary network is restricted because of tension and anxiety our breath cannot support these processes fully. Many illnesses come from not having enough oxygen, not breathing properly; it would seem that the simple act of breathing is something we should all know more about.

Ki meditation teaches a different sort of breathing to what most people are used to; it is based upon deep abdominal breathing, referred to in Korean as *Tan Jon Ho Hup*. Abdominal breathing does not mean that air actually enters your abdomen, it simply means that your abdomen is involved in the process of lowering your diaphragm; you may get the impression that your lower abdomen is filling with air from the bottom up. In this type of breathing we engage a deep part of our body, use the nose during respiration, and are able to inhale more than 2000cc of air per breath.

Ki Breathing – how to perform abdominal breathing (Tan Jon Ho Hup)

<u>Stage One - Ki Breathing</u>

1. Firstly stand at ease, and exhale fully as much air as you can. As we exhale the diaphragm muscle is drawn up and a vacuum is created.

2. Slowly inhale through your nostrils, making no sound. Inhale, gently expanding your ribcage and drawing the diaphragm muscle down. As your diaphragm pulls down, elongating your lungs, you will feel your abdomen expanding outward, creating more space for air to enter your lungs.

   The diaphragm muscle is the floor on which the lungs rest. When this muscle lowers, the lungs expand; the opposite happens when you raise your shoulders in chest breathing – chest breathing once again, reduces your lung capacity.

   Mental imagery can be very useful in helping you to breathe correctly. As you inhale slowly, imagine that air is filling your stomach from the bottom up; imagining this may help you guard against stressing your chest and shoulders, or breathing too shallowly.

3. When you can inhale no more, ensure your chest and shoulders are relaxed, gently contract the perineum or anus, pulling it up slightly and feel that your weight naturally falls to your lower abdomen. Naturally when you contract the perineum, weight should focus on the abdomen area. I will discuss this area of the body in more depth later. The lower abdomen should feel a little tense. This tension is not something external like a body builder doing crunches, but rather an internal lift, and a feeling like everything is being held and supported from the inside.

4. Continue to hold the perineum gently up, and exhale, slowly through the nostrils, raising your diaphragm. For most beginners, the exhalation can provide the hardest challenge as they are often holding excess tension in their chest, shoulders and throat. Try to exhale as slowly as you can, allowing your lungs to empty as much as possible.

5. When all air is exhaled, relax the perineum and start the process again.

For beginners, each inhalation and exhalation may last for about 5 seconds. A few months later you may be able to increase that to 7 seconds, later still maybe 10secs. The longer you practice the longer your breaths can become.

Stage Two – Ki Breathing

Once you are used to this type of breathing, you can also start practicing holding your breath between the inhalation and exhalation. Retention of breathe has a cleansing effect on the body. It gives time for fresh air to mix with stale air in the lungs and permits a greater absorption of oxygen into the blood. Slowing and retaining your breathe also requires and improves concentration skills, forcing you to learn to release more tension from your mind and body.

1. Sit at ease and exhale fully before starting.
2. Slowly inhale through your nostrils as before.
3. When you have inhaled fully, stop breathing and hold your breathe simultaneously raising the perineum as described above. Take care not to tense your shoulders and chest; as you raise the perineum, you should have a feeling that the air is being retained in the abdominal cavity.
4. After the appropriate amount of time (see below) relax and exhale fully.
5. Repeat steps 2-4 for the meditation period.

Most Meditators will inhale for about 7secs, hold for about 7secs and exhale for about 7secs. This means one breath is taking approximately 20secs to complete. As you get better you can improve that to 30 seconds, and later you may be able to extend that to one minute for a simple breath. When breathing, concentrate solely on your breathing being aware of your abdomen and ribcage expanding and contracting. At first this process seems contrived, but as we learn to relax it becomes fluid and natural. As we learn to release unwanted tension from the body, correct breathing becomes largely an unconscious experience.

> **NOTES ON USING THE NOSTRILS:**
>
> Using the nose to breathe can have huge implications for our health: it encourages relaxation, protects our lungs against infection and allergens, and also opens up the capillary network, improving blood supply to the cells
>
> Research teams in Switzerland have discovered that we all have NO (Nitric Oxide) gas in our noses. Through abdominal breathing using the nose to inhale we are able to move this gas into our lungs. The result of this process is the dilation of blood vessels by 30%, which in turn enables oxygen to travel in the blood much better.

Conclusion

Proper breathing is fundamental to Ki Meditation and provides a link to our emotional state. Aside from the necessity of sustaining life, the breath can become an ally which can be used to calm us down, concentrate the mind and help us to achieve clarity of thought. The more stressed and anxious we become the more shallow our breathing. So by learning to control the breathing we can learn to control our emotions. Master Chang would say that, "the tree with heavy roots will remain calm and still, as we will be if we develop strong roots through Ki meditation." Regular Ki breathing should enable you to relax your physical body whilst also giving you a route to calming your mind. Ki breathing has given many people improved physical condition, enhanced concentration, and freedom from anxiety and stress – the building blocks for a long and fulfilling life.

EXPLORING THE TAN JON

The Tan Jon, or abdomen is located two inches below the navel. It is home to the enteric nervous system, 'the brain in the bowel' as Dr. Michael Gershon's refers to it in his book "The Second Brain", (Gershon, 1998) and was the first part of you to be formed in the womb, allowing for feeding from your mother through the umbilical cord. Leonardo De Vinci's famous picture of the Vitruvian man still illustrates beautifully how this area rests at the centre of the human anatomy. Learning to keep our weight low and centralised in this area will increase our power and coordination; likewise, weak muscles in this area contribute to all kinds of problems in the body, the most prevalent being lower back pain. This is your core; and its strength will influence your overall physical and mental state.

Ancient civilisations have instinctively known of the importance of the abdomen. Lao Tsu said, in Chapter Three of the Tao Te Ching, "*The wise rule by emptying hearts and stuffing bellies*". Here 'bellies' refers to our tan jon and is related to our true selves. Have you ever been to a Chinese restaurant and seen the huge statue of the Buddha they often have near the door? His huge belly is unmissable and is your primary focus. The emphasis on the abdomen is not about literally encouraging us to eat more, rather as in Lao Tsu's poems, it is a symbol of an individual's huge spiritual potential.

During abdominal breathing we focus on 'dropping the weight' to this area. As many of us hold tension in our shoulders, this may be felt as a sort of gravitational fall of your body's weight. As this feeling of release becomes more natural we become calmer and more peaceful. A calmer mind enables us to step back from the situations we find ourselves in, and begin to develop a more objective view of ourselves and of the circumstances around us.

What is important to understand then, is that the lower abdomen (Tan Jon) has particular significance. Learning to use this area as a focal point is essential. Through consistent training one begins to develop a feeling of stability and centeredness in the Tan Jon area. Eventually, after long-time practice, the conscious mind will let go and this centralisation will become a continuous unconscious state, requiring less and less effort. So long as we keep breathing shallowly with solely our chests (see the previous chapter on Exploring the Breath), we will never be able to tap into the power of the Tan Jon and we will remain easily influenced and controlled by circumstances around us.

Learning to focus on the tan jon, relaxing your shoulders and chest, and to 'drop your weight' or 'tensing the lower abdomen' while breathing, often provides students with a particular challenge. "What part do I tense?" "How do I relax and tense at the same time?" "What do you mean drop your weight?" "How can I hold my breath while tensing my stomach?" "Why do I have to hold my breath in my abdomen?" The questions that I get on this are never ending, and the only consolation I can give is to persevere. It may also be helpful to reread the section on 'breathing' and below on 'the perineum' from time to time to check that you haven't developed any unhelpful habits. The more you practice the clearer things become; remember, 'practice makes perfect'.

The perineum

As we hold our breath in our lower abdomen, we must 'contract the anus', or pull up the perineum. The dictionary defines the perineum as the bottom part of the pelvis. It is "the region of the abdomen surrounding the urogenital and anal openings".

> **How do we contract the perineum area?**
>
> The easiest analogy is one often used in Pilates and Yoga classes. Imagine you really need to go to the toilet, but hold it in. Your whole lower abdomen should become quite rigid as the abdominal, the lateral and lumbar muscles all engage.
>
> Note: Men contract a spot between the anus and testicles. For women the point of contraction will be the cervix.

Over the past few years sports and fitness professionals have increasingly begun emphasising this area, instructing us to 'engage the core'. Try picking up something heavy. Did you notice what happened to the perineum area? The heavier the object, the more the area contracts. When we focus on this area and gently contract during Ki breathing, it not only helps us to concentrate, but also creates incredible power within the body.

Through the ageing process though, this area loses its elasticity. Problems with premature ejaculation or erectile difficulties often emanate from here. This area can also be problematic for women with urinary difficulties; this is particularly noticeable after child birth as the area has been forcefully stretched.

Ki Meditation breathing can help strengthen this area, thus guarding against difficulties in later life. Focusing on the perineal muscles can improve posture by increasing the stability of the pelvis and spine and can also help sexual health. The torso is the body's centre of power, so the stronger you are in the tan jon area, the easier your life will be.

EXPERIENCING MOVEMENT

Most beginners find sitting meditation exceedingly difficult. The mind often needs about 15 minutes to relax, so persevere even if you find concentration difficult at the start. Adding movement can significantly help concentration by giving the practitioner something on which to focus their attention; this will enable the beginner and intermediate student to meditate for a much longer period of time. When we coordinate mind and body in this way, we become much more aware of the power of our intention. Every motion we make is preceded by the intention to make that motion. Our focused intention then, is the gateway to experiencing the moment and accessing our Ki energy.

On a physical level adding movement also gently exercises the body; it massages the internal organs, stretches the muscles and ligaments, and helps circulate the fluids within the body. In addition to such physical benefits, attaining deeper levels of concentration will enable you to notice the many subtle changes happening in your body. Learning to become centred in the lower abdomen and using the body as a unit powered by the mind's concentration will develop power, stability, coordination and suppleness, qualities associated with youthfulness and well-being. In this way performing Ki exercise will support the body in improving and maintaining itself in healthy condition, allowing you to live life more fully.

What I find when most people start Ki meditation is that they are incredibly out of touch with their own bodies. After years of living primarily in their heads, they often have no idea what they feel like or how they move, or even that they are holding tension in their shoulders, chest or hips. This false sensory perception convinces them that they are relaxed, or that their posture is good. After a few classes students slowly become conscious of the layers of tension, which is the starting point for letting go of stress.

Types of Movement/Postures

Ki exercise may involve various types of movement.
1) **Stretching** the body releases tension, realigns the body and stimulates the body as a whole.
2) Gently **tapping** a body part can stimulate and open the energy in the chosen area.
3) **Rotating** a joint helps loosen and relaxes the area.
4) **Twisting and turning** will help to loosen the body and release tension.
5) **Tensing and releasing** can stimulate, bring energy and/or release tension. This sends fresh oxygenated blood more effectively to all parts of the body.
6) **Shaking** a limb helps to release tension from the body.

Whatever type of movement is being performed, the practitioner should be aware of his posture. Correct posture is the foundation on which proper meditation practice is built. Poor posture will inhibit movement which in turn will occupy the mind. And, as I suggested earlier, our mind will take on the personality of our posture.

When performing the exercises, try to release all muscular stress from the body except that which is needed to perform the motion/posture. As you start to practice you may notice that one side holds more tension than another – the root cause may be anything from an old injury to poor posture or lifestyle habits like the height of your computer screen or a dominant carrying hand. Start by simply noticing these things, and as you begin to stretch consistently you should start to notice improvements in flexibility and your body slowly balancing itself.

When moving, your mind should be calm and relaxed, focusing on the sensory input that each slow movement brings. Movements are accomplished by relaxing and releasing tension in the mind and body, not by relying on physical strength. To aid your focus you could imagine some sort of resistance while you move, as though you were moving through a dense liquid, or heavy fog. Another hint is to imagine you are constantly growing and lengthening through every posture. As you practice, you will start to feel your whole body becoming a condensed source of energy, as you imagine power radiating from the Tan Jon. If you have a tendency toward perfectionism, it can be helpful to think about operating at only 70% capacity. In other words let go of the additional mental stress you may be creating by needing to be perfect; sometimes striving for 100% can cause tension and stress in itself.

There are a hundred or so different postures, more than I can include in this book. What I would like to offer instead is a Ki exercise sequence that the reader can perform. Each exercise should be repeated 2-3 times.

The whole sequence will last approximately 45mins to an hour. If you have less time available you may choose to eliminate some of the postures or simply perform each a single time.

It is essential that you perform Danjon Hohup breathing whilst performing each Ki exercise movement. Unless otherwise specified when inhaling and exhaling always use the nose. Whenever 'hold breath' is indicated between the inhalation and exhalation, create a sensation of the breath continuously sinking and settling to the bottom of the abdomen during the 'hold' period, naturally contracting the perineum. (see the previous section on breathing for more detailed information)

Too much visual stimulus will make it much harder to concentrate. So, when performing exercises, I would recommend that you concentrate your line of vision; some find it helpful to narrow the eyes, as if the eyes combine to make a single eye (The Third Eye).

Cautions

Consult your doctor before starting practice if you have any medical concern, in particular: high blood pressure, pregnancy, heart disease, retinal problems, epilepsy, schizophrenia, joint replacement or other major surgery.

If you feel dizzy or light headed, or if you are feeling upset, this is often caused by holding too much tension across the chest and shoulders. Relax – lie down on your back and breathe normally.

Your flexibility should naturally improve as you release more unwanted tension from your body. Take care not to push a stretch too far; stop the stretch when you feel resistance and focus on relaxing the relevant muscles and tendons.

STANDING POSITION

Natural Stance

Taking a few moments to calm your mind and relax your breath at the start before adding movement to your practice will benefit all subsequent movements.

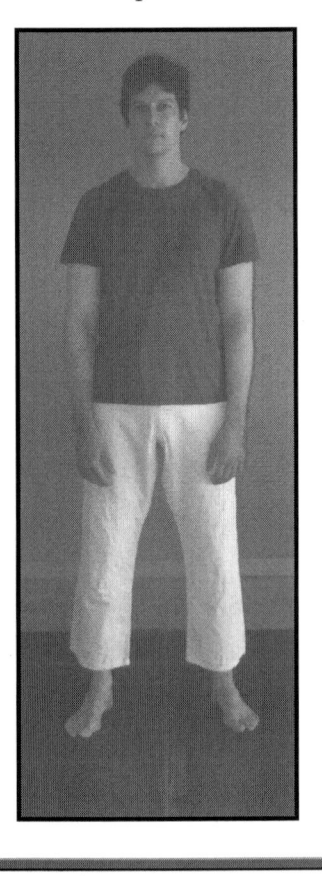

- Simply stand and breathe with no movement. Allow your mind to follow y[our] breath and settle at your lower abdom[en]. Consciously relax and allow your spine [to] lengthen, and your weight to descend natura[lly]. Stand tall with weight low. Standing with [?] shoulder width apart you can feel your f[eet,] hips, shoulders and head naturally align[ed]. Resting on top of each other you can let g[o] unnecessary tensions, confident in knowledge that your body is aligned and abl[e to] support itself.
- Once calm, perform Abdominal breathing 3-5 times.

Benefits
Calms the mind. Promotes relaxation.

Son Sallyio

The term 'son sallyio' can be translated as 'make your hand alive with Ki'. Spread your fingers wide and imagine energy emanating from the fingertips. This hand position is used in many of the subsequent movements.

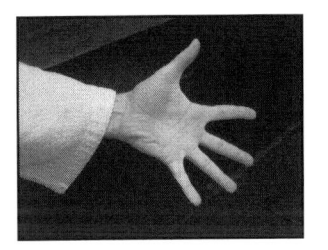

Son Sallyio increases blood circulation to the fingers, increasing mental clarity and enhancing the transport of energy throughout the body. Hands will become both stronger and more sensitive.

Hand circles to abdomen

- From standing position, inhale slowly as you gently bring your hand (Son sallyio) to rest in front of your abdomen. Take care to keep the shoulders low and use the back muscles to move.
- Hold breath in your lower stomach, then exhale as you return to starting position.

<u>Variations</u>

(1) Move both hands simultaneously.
(2) Allow hands to rest at chest height.
(3) Raise hands all the way up above your head.

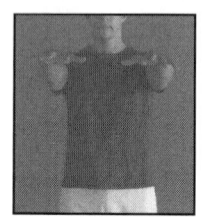

Benefits

Opens up the shoulders. Stretches arms & upper back. Son Sallyio will strengthen hands and promote concentration.

Side Lean

- From standing position place one hand, with thumb forward, on your waist.
- As you inhale, raise your hand (son sallyio) over your head, reaching upward to lengthen your body out. Resist the temptation to look at your hand; instead, keep forward facing, with elbows locked and your head up (don't let your chin sink). Continue the motion by leaning sideways. Feel the stretch down the curved side of your body. You can increase the stretch by pushing your hips to the opposite side of the lean.
- Hold in your lower abdomen.
- Exhale while returning to the start position.

Benefits

Improves the flexibility of the spine and strengthens the core.

Hands either way

- Step into a wide right stance. Keeping your left knee gently locked, turn your right foot and leg directly toward the right and your left foot at a 45 degree angle (Your heels should be on the same line). Bend your right knee so it is directly over your heel, and the thigh is parallel to the floor, simultaneously extending your arms both directions (son sallyio) as you slowly inhale. *It is very important that your knee does not push out beyond your heel, adjust the width of your stance if you needed.*
- Hold in your lower abdomen.
- Exhale while returning to the start position.

Benefits
Increases strength and flexibility in the hips. Improves balance and core strength. Tones muscles on the sides of the torso. Stretches adductor muscles. Strengthens the legs and muscles of the gluteus.

Wrists up

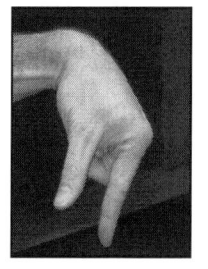

- From standing position, bend your wrists to 90 degrees. Extend your first finger and thumb, while curling the remaining fingers into your palm. The fingers should feel like they are pulling towards your body, and the wrist should be tense.
- As you inhale, raise your wrists up and forward to shoulder height. Take care not to tense the neck and shoulders. 
- Hold. Exhale and return to starting position.

Variations

(1) Do one wrist at a time.
(2) Bring wrists out to the side.

Benefits

Strengthens wrists and forearms. Improves concentration.

Wrist Sweep & Push

- From standing position, inhale whilst stepping one foot forward and raising your bent wrists above your head. *Note: Feet should be slightly wider than hips, and toes pointed forward. The knee should be directly over the heel.*
- Sweep elbows and wrists back into your chest. Feel like you are drawing your shoulder blades together as you push your chest forward. Make sure your wrists and elbows are held tight to your sides.
- Hold. Exhale as you return to starting position.

Variations

(1) Push forward with your hands, as if pushing wall back.

Benefits

Stretches calf, wrists, forearm and chest. Strengthens thigh and muscles of the gluteus. Opens the chest. Strengthens arms and shoulders.

Clasp and push

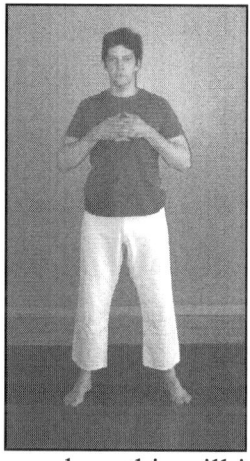

- Clasp your hands together on your chest.
- Breathe in, pushing your hands forward with palms facing out, and looking at the back of your hands. Have the feeling that you are sending lighting bolts out of your palms; this will increase your stretch and aid concentration.
- Hold.
- Return your hands to the original position as you breathe out.

Variations
(1) Turn to one side
(2) Push upwards
(3) Push up while turning to one side.

Benefits

Stretches wrist, forearm and upper back muscles.

Turning motion will further stretch abdominal obliques and quadratus lumborum.

Forward Bend - all the way down

Please take care with this stretch if you are particularly tight or new to this sort of movement. Always listen to your body and stop if you feel any discomfort.

- Lock your fingers behind your head. Before you bend forward, ensure that your body is fully lengthened up.
- Inhale through your nostrils. Stop breathing; hold your breath in your abdomen.
- Bend your trunk forward, leading the bend with your stomach and hips, not your head. Try to keep your back flat, not hunched over.
- Hold. Then, exhale as you return to the original position.  

Variations

(1) Twist toward your knee before bending your trunk.

Benefits

Stretches the spine, hamstrings, calves and hips. Strengthens the upper body and back, quadriceps and knees.

92

KNEELING POSITION

Energising breath

Note: Exhaling while bending over squeezes air out of the abdomen. Inhaling as you sit up, will draw air easily into the abdomen.

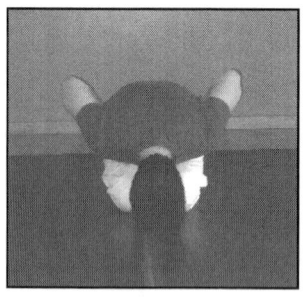

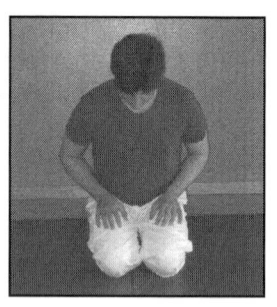

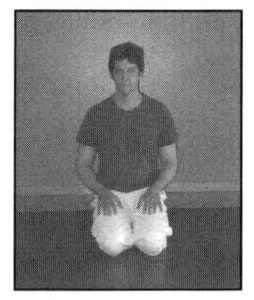

- Start with your head down on your lap, and hands resting gently on your thighs.
- Inhale slowly as you rise up.
- Immediately tense the abdomen and contract the anus and breathe out, slowly falling down to the start position again.
- Repeat this 5-10 times
- Repeat again for 5-10 times but this time hold the breath in your lower abdomen after inhaling.

Benefits
Restores energy. Improves concentration. Calms the mind.

Head down

- Starting from kneeling position with hands clasped around your head, inhale slowly through your nostrils.
- Hold.
- Looking at your navel, slowly bend forward creating a tight ball on the floor. Feel your chin compress into your throat, while your spine and back muscles stretch out.
- Exhale as you return to starting position.

Variations
1. Turn toward one side.

Notes:

Some people may find the kneeling position quite uncomfortable. Provided you do not have an injury you should persevere with this posture. Initially however it might help to place a rolled up towel or other bolster between your buttocks and your heels; this may take some of the pressure off your ankles and knees.

Benefits
Stretches neck, shoulders and back, elongating the spine. Compression of your chin into the throat will massage the thyroid gland. Kneeling position stretches the quads and ankles.

Leaning backward

- Separate your knees and place your hands back.
- As you inhale raise your stomach to the ceiling compressing the spine. Allow your head and neck to relax.
- Hold in your lower abdomen.
- As you exhale return to the original position.

Benefits
Strengthens back; stretches shoulders, chest, stomach, quadriceps, hip flexors and ankles. Stimulates thymus gland (supports immune function).

LYING POSITION
(FACE DOWN)

Breath in, push up

- Lie on your stomach, with hands under your face – fingertips slightly touching.
- Inhale and hold your breathe, dropping your weight and contracting your anus.
- Slowly raise your upper body, until your arms and spine are fully stretched and you are looking at the ceiling. Take care not to retract the head too much, and thus throwing the spine out of alignment- the spine should form a natural arc (no crease in the back of the neck).
- Hold in this position, then relax and exhale as you return to the starting position.

Variations

1) Breathe in, as you push up.
2) Raise your lower legs as you push up. Then rotate your ankles as you hold your breathe.

Benefits

Improves the backward extension of the spine. Stretches chest, shoulders and abs. Strengthens spine, arms, wrists and buttocks. Stimulates thymus gland (supports immune function).

Bow exercise

- Lie on your stomach. Bend your knees and grasp your ankles from the outside.
- Inhale and hold the breath in your lower abdomen.
- Gently lift your head, chest and knees off the floor, trying to keep the knees approximately 6-8 inches apart. You should feel as if you are resting on the soft area of your stomach.
- Hold in this position, then relax and exhale as you return to the starting position.

Benefits

Stretches the entire front of the body, ankles, thighs and groins, abdomen and chest, and throat, and deep hip flexors. Strengthens the back muscles. Stimulates thymus gland (supports immune function).

Reverse Stretch

As you move to the sitting position, take advantage to stretch your back and shoulders.

- Keeping your arms fully extended forward, lower your chest and waist to the floor. Hold. Keep your upper body engaged, while your lower body fully relaxes.
- Alternately, place one arm at a 90 degree angle to the shoulders. Turn your head the other direction. Hold

Benefits

Resting pose that stretches hips, quadriceps and ankles releases back and neck, and increases blood flow to the brain. Stretches sides of torso and arms (latissimus dorsi, teres major and serratus anterior).

SITTING POSITION

Knee over

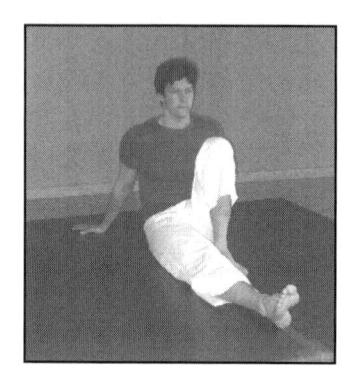

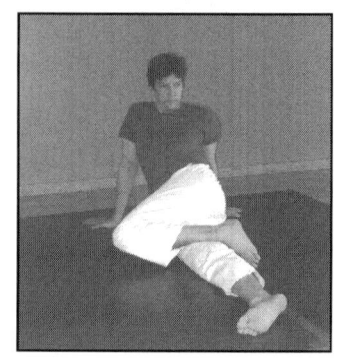

- Place your hands behind you, and have your legs outstretched.
- As you inhale draw in one foot, raising the knee up.
- Hold your breath in your lower abdomen.
- Twist your waist, touching your knee to the opposite side floor.
- Hold. Exhale while returning to the start position.

Benefits

Promotes flexibility of the lower extremities. Stretches lower back and side of hip.

Leg over and Twist

- Bend the right leg and place the right foot over the left leg, near the left knee. Bend the left leg and place it under your hip.
- Inhale and hold the breath in your lower abdomen, then tightly grip your raised knee.
- As you exhale return to the original position.
- Do both sides.

Variation

As you inhale, maintain a straight but relaxed spine. At the same time rotate your wrist around your body, keep it shoulder height. Keep your gaze on your hand in order to turn your body as one unit.

Benefits

Twists spine from top to bottom, stretching neck, shoulders, spine and hips. Increases circulation to all spinal nerves, calming nervous system. Stretches gluteus and hamstrings. Improves trunk flexibility.

Holding tight to knee

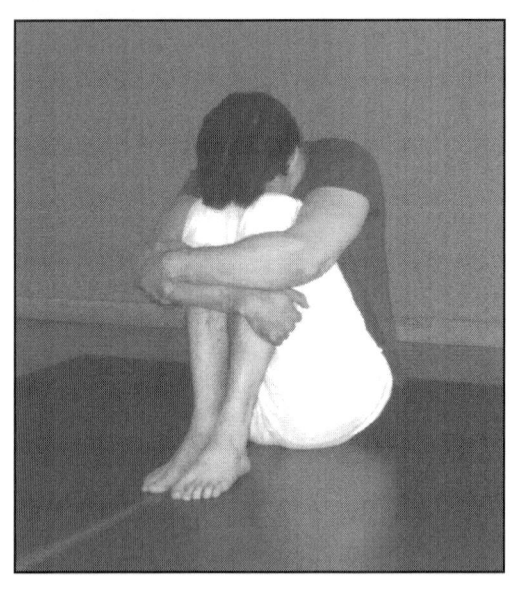

- Sit with knees tucked into your body, and arms clasped around knees.
- Inhale slowly, ensuring your spine is lengthening up.
- When you have finished inhaling, drop into a hunched position, bringing your forehead to your knees, whilst looking at your navel. Clasp the knees as tight as you can, and hold the breath in your lower abdomen.
- Exhale as you relax back to the starting position.

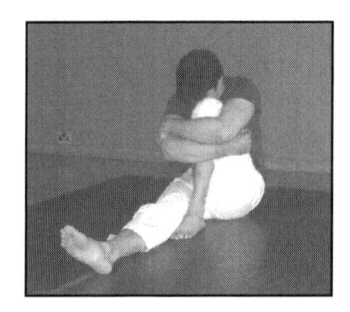

Variations

1. Clasp one knee at a time.
2. Perform in lying down position.

Benefits

Promotes full body relaxation through tension and release. This is also a good lower back exercise designed to strengthen the spine, muscles around the abs, vertebrae, tailbone and kidneys.

Lying Position
(Face up)

Chin to chest

- From lying position, clasp your hands behind your head.
- Inhale and hold in your lower abdomen.
- Raise head, shoulders and chest off the ground. (Keep middle and lower back on the floor) Ensure your legs are straight and toes pointed.
- Exhale as you return to starting position.

    Variations
    1. Lean to one side
    2. Raise Legs – 'V' shape

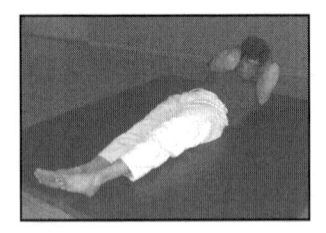

Benefits

Stretches neck, shoulder, abdominals and upper back muscles. Massages thyroid gland.

Variation 2 will also strengthen lower abdominals, quadriceps, hip flexors and lower back.

Knee up

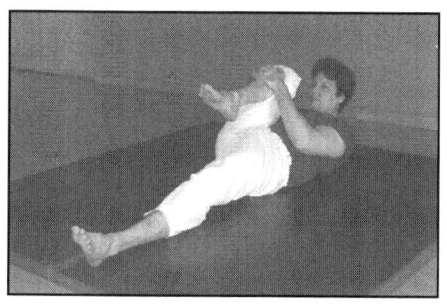

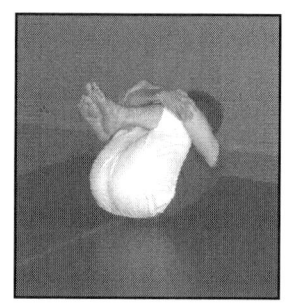

- From lying position, bend your right knee, and clasp your hands a few inches below the kneecap.
- As you inhale draw your knee in to your armpit avoiding the ribcage.
- As you hold in your lower abdomen, bring your head up to touch your forehead to your knee.
- Exhale as you return to starting position.

    Variations
    1. Raise the left knee
    2. Raise both knees

Note: Do the right side first to massage the ascending colon ,the left will then focus on the descending colon. Grabbing elbows and holding both knees massages the transverse colon & compress the digestive system.

Benefits

Improves digestion by compressing and massaging the colon. Strengthens arms, improves hip flexibility and firms abs and thighs. Stretches Gluteus Maximus and back/spinal muscles.

Holding Ankle raise hips

- From lying position, bring your knees up and grab your ankles.
- As you inhale raise your hips to the sky, maximizing the stretch.
- Hold in your lower abdomen.
- Exhale as you return to starting position.

Benefits
Strengthens the muscles of the gluteus and hamstrings, quadriceps and knees. Stretches the chest, neck, shoulders and spine. Stimulates thymus gland (supports immune function).

Tapping

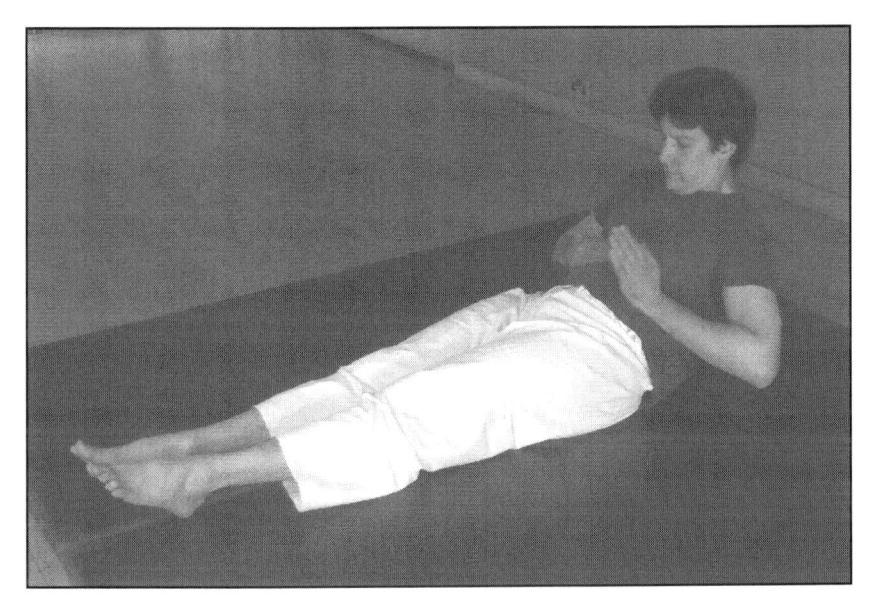

- Lie on your back with hands resting on your stomach.
- Slowly inhale and hold in your lower abdomen.
- Raise head and gently tap or rub the whole area above the pubic bone to below the rib cage.
- Exhale as you return to the starting position.

Benefits

Brings energy. Strengthens the immune system. Alleviates nervousness

Total Relaxation Breath

- Lying on the floor with knees raised and ankles held, inhale slowly.
- When you have finished inhaling quickly tense your whole body; raise up off the floor.
- Hold
- Slowly exhale whilst relaxing the body gradually from the toes up.
- Repeat 4-5 times.
- On the final repetition exhale fast out the mouth relaxing the body quickly and dropping into corpse position. Imagine your body getting heavier and heavier. You may find you fall asleep.

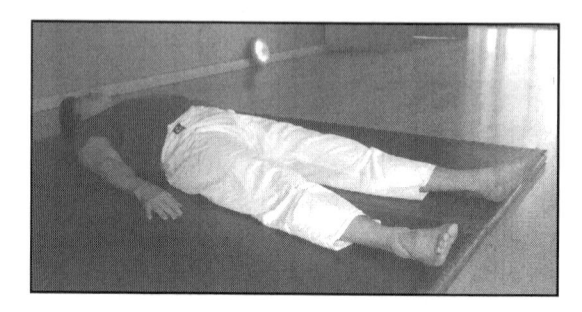

Benefits

This movement can release aches and pains from the body, whilst regenerating your energy and mental focus in a very short space of time.

EXPERIENCING SITTING

There is no better way to become more consciously aware of your present circumstances than through the exercise of stillness found in meditation practice. From the outside it would appear that meditation would be an easy pursuit: an excuse for the idle, an escape for the industrious, a chance to rest and recharge, reconsider arguments or perhaps frustrations. Meditation, however, is anything but easy. We are so conditioned that much of our daily existence is lived mulling over the past or lamenting the future. But full awareness and the beauty of life is found right now, in this present moment. Meditation is not a time-out, but a time-in; dropping into stillness is anything but passive. Our challenge is to release the grip of years of conditioning so that we can be fully present. Meditation is wakefulness. And true wakefulness brings both power and freedom.

Master Chang tells the story of the elephant calf who was tied to a stake when small and later grew to full adulthood, still thinking he was trapped and restricting his own movements. The process of meditation allows us to see where we are 'tying ourselves to a stake' and then cast aside the beliefs and constructs that are trapping us.

Master Chang also speaks about a place where farmers have a particular technique for catching monkeys. "They put fruit in a jar and place it outside in the sun. The jar has a small neck, large enough for the monkey to place his arm in, but as soon as he grips the fruit, the arm muscle expands and becomes too large for the neck of the jar. The monkey doesn't want to be caught, but unwilling to let go of the fruit, he allows himself to be easily captured."

When we find ourselves at the height of a negative emotion, treating someone without compassion or craving something, the 'monkey mind' is taking over. Like the monkey attached to the fruit, or the elephant fixed to the spot, we too cling to our delusions thinking they will give us what we crave. True freedom then comes from putting our judgements aside and letting go of false realities. As the subconscious mind cannot distinguish between reality and imagination, our thoughts and feelings are at the heart of any transformation we wish to make.

Once our body has been warmed and stretched and our mind settled through the practice of Ki Exercise, we are ready to begin sitting meditation.

Sitting meditation posture

1. Ideally the practitioner sits in full or half lotus position, a cross-legged sitting posture with feet resting on the opposing thighs. Such a sitting position helps to promote maximum awareness of the lower torso base and tan jon. If this is uncomfortable he should experiment with placing a bolster or cushion underneath the hip in order to keep himself upright. Sitting cross legged is also acceptable, but take care not to hunch or collapse

your back. Whatever the position, your posture should feel balanced and unforced. I often refer to it as *dignified*, in other words neither slouched nor rigid.

In the West we are not as used to sitting in this manner so the time spent in this position should be built up gradually.

2. Touch the middle finger and thumb together in order to create a circle. In meditation practice, hand positions are used to regulate and balance the flow of subtle energy throughout the body; it could be said that the hand gesture has the power to achieve that which it represents. This particular position is popular among Buddhist practitioners and is said to promote awareness of the moment thus making one more patient.

3. Rest the hands, palm facing upwards, on the knees. Resting your forearms in this manner can help prevent the habit of tensing your shoulders, whilst also allowing you to keep the weight focused downward.

4. Slightly wet your lips with your tongue to prevent them from drying during meditation practice.

5. Partially close the eyes in order to stop distraction. But keep them slightly open in order to keep you awake and alert. As I sit, I am aware that I can see the mat under my feet, but not the person in front of me. Seeing too much will make it much harder to concentrate.

6. Finally, smile.

When we soften the face, the rest of the body will often follow. Dr William Fry at Stanford University found that the smile stimulates the brain to naturally release chemicals that inhibit infection and

lessen pain. It also reduces stress related hormones and increases heart rate and blood circulation. So by smiling during meditation you will tap into a lot more positive energy.
7. Now perform Danjon hohup breathing as before.

Seated meditation posture
1. Sit on a chair with back and hips supported comfortably. Consciously encourage your back muscles to release any tension, thinking of your head moving up as your spine lengthens, but allowing your weight to settle down and release through your sitting bones.
2. Place feet on the floor, hip width apart, this will allow your legs to relax while also connecting you to the earth.
3. Place one hand atop the other and touch the thumbs together. This hand position is said to symbolise the Buddha in meditation and promotes concentration; you will find that it naturally helps to relax and balance the upper body when seated.
4. Rest hands in this position next to abdomen with shoulders relaxed.
5. Slightly wet your lips with your tongue to prevent them from drying during meditation practice.
6. Close the eyes in order to stop distraction. But keep them slightly open in order to keep you awake.
7. Finally, smile.
8. Now perform Danjon hohup breathing as before.

Aids to concentration when sitting

Virtually everyone finds it hard to concentrate at the start. Focusing on the rise and fall of the breath and counting as you the inhale/exhale are both simple techniques that you can experiment with in order to hone your concentration skills. Other meditation schools may ask students to focus on the sound of a gong, stare at a candle flame, or chant a mantra repeatedly. I'm also familiar with one style that teaches practitioners to name their mental chatter, "Thinking", which reduces its power and allows the student to return to focusing on the breath and the moment. All these are excellent concentration tools.

Sitting Duration

If you have never meditated before, a 5 or 10 minute sitting meditation may prove quite challenging. On average though it takes about 15 minutes to still the mind, so if you can manage 15-20 minutes that would be preferable. Later, when you are more experienced, you can lengthen that to 45mins or an hour.

Best Time to Meditate

The most ideal time to meditate is before noon, as energy rises in morning, and falls after 12-noon. From my own experience I have found that when I meditate not long after waking, my whole day seems to benefit from taking that little bit of time to stop. But, that's not going to be practical for everyone's lifestyle. In reality the best time is going to be a time that you are able to do it. Creating a habit of always meditating at a certain time will also make it more likely to happen.

Training Hard

When I first started Ki meditation training with Master Chang a good twenty years ago, he would walk around the meditation room with a big bamboo stick ready to abruptly stir those students who had fallen asleep or allowed their posture to collapse. Realising this approach was less suited to our modern western lives Master Chang has since stopped this practice, though it is still followed regularly in many Zen monasteries even today. Some may call this practice 'hard training', but to me hard training is something quite different.

The more regularly we practice the more we can gain from Ki Meditation. Master Chang says we should always, "be serious, train hard." But that doesn't mean that we start adding to our stress levels in a desperate attempt to be perfect. Training hard means being committed to discovering our true potential and embracing and encouraging our own personal growth. It also means deepening our understanding of the world around us and how we are connected to one another and the world around us.

Someone new came to Ki class one Monday recently. It was just him and me at the start of the class, so I chatted for a little bit. Half way through Ki exercise he looked very stressed. I asked him if he was okay. He said that he had seen us many times through the windows and it seemed so easy, but actually he was finding the whole thing very difficult and was noticeably getting more and more stressed by this. "Is it normal to be struggling to move and breathe?" he asked. I told him that it was new and different - that I was asking him to step outside of his normal way of being, to let go of things that he might be holding on to. I told him that I would be quite surprised if he didn't find that initially quite stressful. "Oh really!" he responded. He physically relaxed in an instant. "So it's okay to find it difficult!"

In Ki Class a few days later someone told me about the nephew of a friend of his. The boy had a pronounced stutter, so he asked his friend about it. Apparently up until a year ago the child (5yrs old) had not spoken at all. He would make a little bit of noise and then go crazy, breaking things and hitting things. They taught him sign language. As soon as he was able to say what he wanted, he relaxed. As soon as he relaxed, he started to talk.

Ki training can be more challenging than it may seem. Regular training takes patience and perseverance, but the practice is ongoing and should be seen as a journey to be enjoyed, not merely the bit before you get to your destination.

Concluding thoughts

Continued comprehensive training in Ki Meditation involves one's whole being both inside and out. As your practice improves you will find that your body becomes softer, more supple and more coordinated; your powers of perception and reaction will also become sharpened; and you will find yourself seeing, understanding and being able to respond to situations with a greater awareness and clarity. Regular practitioners will notice a reduction in stress and anxiety levels, a lowering of high blood pressure and an improvement in breathing related problems. As stress suppresses the immune system you may find that you start getting less colds and flu outbursts. Concentration and creativity will improve and thinking will become clearer. You will become more aware of your thoughts and emotions and be able to notice what triggers negative states of mind; this will dispel any victim mentality and bring choice back into your life. Meditation practice has also been known to reduce the urge to smoke, take drugs or participate in other addictive or avoidance behaviour, because of the impact it has on relieving the stress and anxiety that often underpins such behaviour.

Much of the real benefits of Ki meditation come from long term regular practice. From the first time you sit down to train however, you will begin to benefit from Ki Meditation practice. Our psychological states and tension patterns however are individual to us, so what it means to me to let go and experience my true self will be totally different from what it means to you. If you continue to practice you will experience more of the benefits you need at whatever pace is most appropriate to you. Some people notice changes immediately, while others meditate for months and feel that nothing much is happening. If the latter is the case with you I would recommend that you ask family and friends if they have noticed any changes in you themselves – sometimes it is other people who notice things first. As long as you meditate regularly, you can trust that transformation is happening. It is like the process of dyeing a cloth back to it's original white colour. Each time you dye it, it gets a little brighter, until finally the cloth is a clean, pure white once again.

Ki training takes practice and perseverance. Like most things in life, getting the most out of Ki training means making it part of your daily experience. For some that will constitute quite a change to their normal routine; but if we recall the philosophical guiding concepts we will know that action is required to change old patterns of behaviour. Developing any new routine requires an adjustment period of maybe a few months to build up that new habit. Creating good habits now though will transform our future; or as Master Chang would say, "We are today what we did repeatedly".

A final thought? Remember that to become a master of Ki does not mean that you should curb who you are, or suppress your personality; instead you become "more you" – an authentic, energetic, compassionate and powerful version of yourself.

셋
set / (3) three

MYTHS, LEGENDS & STORIES

A COLLECTION OF MASTER CHANG'S STORIES

I have enjoyed Master Chang tell these stories hundreds of times. Writing them now, feels like welcoming back an old friend who brings new wisdom. The aim of this sort of story telling is to provoke the student to question how he/she sees the world, and awaken a new insight.

THE TEA MASTER

An old man bumped into a samurai in a crowd by mistake and the samurai challenged him to a duel. This old man was actually a Tea Master who knew nothing of fighting, so he went to see Miyomoto Musashi who many had gone to for sword fighting lessons.

When he met Musashi, the Tea Master simply asked, "How do I die with honour?" Musashi was surprised, most people came to him to learn how to kill, "who are you?", he asked.

"I am nobody", he responded, "just a Tea Master", said the man. "So, make me Tea", replied Musashi.

The Tea Master, though only hours away from death made tea, and did it so single-mindedly that Musashi told him to leave because he could already die with honour.

Time for the duel arrived. The Samurai was already there and was frustrated, "so you finally decided to come, lets fight!" The Tea Master said nothing, but bowed. He placed his sword down and bowed again. Finally he lifted his sword above his head, and stayed there, unmoving.

Seeing his composure the Samurai began to shake. "Maybe I've chosen the wrong opponent," he thought. As the sun reflected on the Tea Master's Sword he saw red. "Is that my blood?, am I already dead?" Finally the samarai dropped to the floor apologising, "I am so sorry Master, please forgive me". The Tea Master said nothing, just collected up his belongings. The Samuari started running after him, "please take me as your student", he begged. After much persistence the Tea Master agreed.

The Tea Master taught the samurai how to control his mind. The samurai knew how to fight but that was all.

THE BEST WARRIOR

The mayor of the city wanted to find the best warrior. Three warriors were asked to the mayor's house for dinner, each about 20 minutes after the other. A young man was asked to hide behind the entrance gate, and when each entered to "thwack" him with a stick. The first warrior entered and as he stepped over the threshold was struck down unconscious. Twenty minutes later the second warrior approached. As he came close the young man brought down his sword but this time the warrior was too fast. He stepped away, blocked and struck, pinning the young man to the wall. "What are you doing, I could kill you!" The young man apologised and the warrior entered. The last warrior came towards the gate and stopped. "I don't know who is behind the gate but please do not play tricks like this, please step out." The young man came from behind the gate with his sword down. This was the best warrior.

THE MOULA TEACHES HIS DISCIPLES

A friend bumped into a Moula who was searching on his hands and knees in the gutter. "What are you doing?" the friend asked. Moula explained that he was searching for a key he had lost. So, the friend got onto his hands and knees and began to help Moula look for the lost item. After a while the friend questioned, "Moula, where did you lose your key?" Moula replied, "Inside my house". The friend was shocked, "then why are you searching outside?" "Because the sun is outside;" replied Moula, "my house is too dark and I can not see anything."

WON HYO

As was the way at that time, Won Hyo decided to travel to China for enlightenment. The journey was long and arduous. Along the way he took a nap; early in the morning he awoke with an incredible thirst. It was dark, but blindly feeling around his body he found a cup with water. He drank the water and drifted back to sleep feeling much relieved.

In the morning he awoke to find that the cup which he drank from was actually a human skull. And the water that he drank was stagnant.

He immediately felt nauseous and vomited.

At that point he had a realization. Won Hyo exclaimed, "Last night I thought this was water and it quenched my thirst. This morning I see that it is something else, so I am relating to it quite differently and am sick to my stomach. Therefore, mind makes everything, and without mind everything is empty."

With this great insight Won Hyo realized he did not have to travel to China. Instead, he remained in Korea, resigning from the priesthood to teach as a layman.

Won Hyo's astonishment at his unknowing actions and the power of the human mind to transform reality continue to be relevant even today.

KYONG HO

A master monk (*Kyong Ho*) was begging with his novice monk. They were given a bag of rice which the novice monk was instructed to carry. He complained to his Master, "Oh Master it is so heavy". At that time a young woman walked past with a water jug on her head. The Master ran over and kissed her. She was so shocked that the jug fell off and smashed on the ground. Within a matter of seconds her family had seen what had happen and started to come after the pair. The Master and novice monk had no time to think, but ran as fast as they could in order to escape. Finally they were out of the village and safe. The master turned to his student, "how heavy is your bag?"... The novice monk replied... "What bag, I forgot I was carrying it!"

THE COCKEREL FIGHT

One day, a noble man brought one of his cockerels to a professional trainer to train the cockerel to fight better.

10 days later the owner came back and asked, how is my cockerel doing?"

"Your cockerel is physically strong and big, but the other cockerels cackle at him he does the same thing as the other cockerels do, he is often frightened by the shadow of other cockerels and he is boasty and showy, strutting around thinking I am strong - so still long to go."

So the owner came back 10days and asked the same question.

"No your cockerel is strong but cackling too much still he is afraid of shadow a little better but still emotionally very like other cockerels"

Another 10 days came back is ready, "no one problem still he wants pacing chin up I am strong like that"

Another 10days – "Yeah your cockerel is ready to fight",

"Then how has he changed?"

"Now he is very clam, other cockerels try to provoke but your cockerel still calm moving slow like that"

The owner was wondering, "what do you mean by that, surely a good fighter must be strong - how come my cockerel is so gentle? How can he fight?"

"Other cockerels come near to your cockerel to provoke him, but still not influenced. After they try a few times they get scared and run away."

The Monk who can be cut into 10 Pieces

During the 1950's the Chinese invaded Tibet. All the monks had to flee to the hills before the armies stormed the monasteries. The army went to one monastery, however, and discovered one monk still there meditating in front of the Buddha. The soldiers were scared of him so went back to their general to report what had happened. The General decided to see for himself what was happening. Upon arriving, the General said, "I can cut you up into ten pieces why do you sit there and do nothing?" The monk shouted, "because I am the man you can cut up into ten pieces". The general realised he could not kill him spiritually and bowed to the monk with respect.

Being the best Karateka

A young man turned up at the school of a famous martial arts instructor. Upon arriving, he told the Master that he wanted to become his student and be the best martial artist in Japan. He asked the master, "How long should I train under you?"

"Ten Years," replied the master.

The young man complained. "Ten years is a long time; but what if I train twice as hard as your other students?"

The Master thought for a moment and replied, "20years".

The young man was confused, "20years? But what if I practice every day and night with all my effort?"

After a pause the master replied, "Then 30 years".

Even more confused, the young man enquired, "Why do you say it will take longer every time I say that I will train harder?".

The master smiled. "It is clear. When one eye is fixed upon your destination, there is only one eye left with which to find the way"

THE BEAUTIFUL FLOWER

One day a sword master was walking in his garden. As always his student walked behind him holding the master's sword atop a cushion. The master stopped for a moment to ponder the beauty of a flower. As he did this he suddenly felt the air of death. He immediately turned round; behind him was only his student bowing his head as usual. Confused the Master retreated to his meditation room. After a few days of meditation the student became concerned for his master and asked him what was wrong. The Master explained what had happened and added, "I have trained for many years to identify danger but for some reason I can't explain why I felt such danger that day." After the Master explained the student looked shocked and fell to his knees exclaiming, "Master forgive me. When you were looking at the flower I thought, 'my Master looks so small, perhaps I could take this sword and kill him'. Please forgive me." The master, pleased to understand what had happened just smiled and returned to his garden.

넷
net / (4) four

APPENDICES

APPENDIX 1: GLOSSARY

Epoché

A concept developed by Aristotle, the Greek word *epoché* means, *put your judgements aside.* In other words we should not be influenced by circumstance; we should not be influenced by *Sam*.

Hapkido

Hapkido is a Korean martial art of self-defence which unleashes inner power through coordination of mind and body. The term Hapkido is derived from three Korean words.

Hap – The coordination of mind and body

Ki – The life force, inner energy and power created and manifested from 'Hap'

Do – The self-controlled and disciplined life necessary to create 'Hap' and 'Ki'.

Hapkido is a complete martial art which utilizes kicks, punches, twists, throws and pressure point techniques to subdue an opponent without causing serious injuries.

Karma

Karma comes from a concept of Indian philosophy meaning action. It is a part of living and cannot be avoided. It is something which we cause, not which is forced upon us by other people. If we can control our thoughts, our speech and our actions then we can change our Karma.

Because of the principle of Karma we should not judge people in the same way simply because they do the same thing at the same time. Each person has different Karma, different motivation, which forces them to act.

To clarify Karma, firstly one should empty one's mind; Ki Meditation is a fantastic tool to help us with this. Negative Karma can then be cleansed by positive action and positive thought. Provided our new habits are stronger than our old habits then we don't have to worry.

Our destiny will be determined by the quality of the content we put into our container.

Ki-boon

Ki-boon refers to a partial portion of our Ki; it is a psycho emotional reaction (a feeling or state of mind), and a state of feeling at a particular time (our mood).

Mushim

No-mind or mindfulness. It is a state of being fully alive, an ongoing expression of pure human nature.

Mu-Wei: No-action

Lao Tzu in his famous book The Tao Te Ching, spoke about Mu-wei. Chapter thirty-seven starts,

> Tao abides in non-action,
> Yet nothing is left undone.

In other words it is a state where actions are in accord with nature. Doing something unnaturally creates problems; it creates karma. Mu-wei is acting in Mushim; it is about getting out of one's own way: nothing doing but everything done.

Sam

The Korean word "Sam" and the Sanskrit word "lachksana" have a similar meaning. They refer to sign, symbol, price tag or visual value. When we become influenced or attached to *Sam*, our mind becomes corrupted and we can no longer view things as they are. It is as if we view the world through a filter which disrupts our vision, and our interpretation or judgement of the world becomes distorted.

Son Sallyio

Son sallyio means to 'make your hand alive with Ki'; the fingers are spread wide and energy emanates from the fingertips.

APPENDIX 2: SPECIALISED BREATHING TECHNIQUES

The standard abdominal breathing (Danjon Hohup) explained previously improves the entire body and mind. For those wanting to specialize further though, the method of breathing can be adjusted to focus on particular issues.

There doesn't appear to be any comprehensive scientific research that validates the health benefits claimed below. I read an interesting paper however from researchers at the Association for Applied Psychophysiology & Biofeedback. They reported that each nostril actually houses different nerves which stimulate separate areas of the brain; further mention was also made concerning the mouth, and how using the mouth to inhale will mean that air circumvents the warming effect produced by the nasal cavity. (Telles & Naveen) Until more thorough research can be conducted, I would encourage the reader to perform his own experiments, learning to notice the subtle changes he himself experiences. Just last week I cured my own sore throat by performing clenched teeth breathing (see below) on the tube before going to teach a Ki Meditation class.

Each type of breathing listed can be performed 10-15 times. Unless otherwise specified the breath should be held in the abdomen between inhalation and exhalation, whilst naturally contracting the perineum. (See the main text for more detailed information)

1. **Alternate Nostril breathing**

Block your right nostril with your right hand thumb and breathe in through the left nostril. After you have breathed in fully, block the left nostril with your right hand ring finger, dropping your head to your chest and holding as normal in your abdomen. On the exhale, release your thumb, breathing out of the right nostril. On the next breath, inhale through the right nostril and exhale through the left. Continue switching nostrils in this manner on each breath. Halfway through the set change to using your left hand. Doing at least 15-20 times is ideal (10mins +). If you continue, you should find yourself perspiring after about 20 mins.

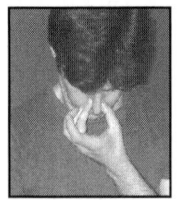

- Emotional stability
- Facial beauty
- Good voice
- Improves appetite
- Will help to save up energy

We naturally breathe through one nostril at a time, each taking it's turn for a few hours. With this in mind it shouldn't be surprising if one nostril feels a little more 'natural'.

2. **Right Nostril Breathing**

As above (Alternate nostril breathing) but breathe solely through the right nostril.

- Improves thinking power

- Cures digestion problems
- Helps nose/eye problems.

3. **Left Nostril exhale breathing**

Inhale through both nostrils. Block your right nostril only as you drop your head to your chest and hold in the abdomen. On the exhalation use only the left nostril.

- Headaches
- Asthma
- Stomach
- Strengthens lung

4. **Tongue curled breathing**

Inhale through' the mouth with your tongue curled. Exhale through' both nostrils.

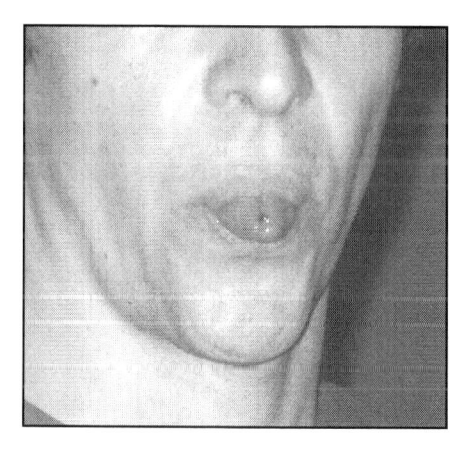

- If thirsty will be able to prolong w/o water
- Helps chronic digestion problems
- Improves endurance
- Saves oxygen (through' this breathing some people who were buried alive could survive – also can help calm Asthma sufferers)

5. Clenched teeth breathing

Breathe in through' clenched teeth, exhale through' nostrils.

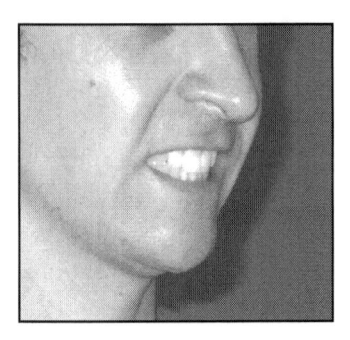

- For throat infections
- Takes care of mucous
- Strengthens stomach
- Cures nose & chest diseases
- Relieves headache – tension at the back of the neck

6. Reverse Breathing with fast Exhale

Breathe in through the nose drawing the stomach in and & raising the diaphragm (may make noise). Without holding, immediately exhale bending the body over as if bowing forcefully.

- When really tired & can't think right away allows to recover energy
- Purifies body & brain
- Bronchitis and Asthma
- Stuffy nose – right away cures

7. Purification Breathe

Inhale through both nostrils, exhale though the mouth either as one long breath or in spurts which get longer - -- --- ---- ----- ------.

- Gets rid of toxins
- Aids immune system
- Relieves headaches
- Relieves colds

- Aids rest
- Good for your voice.

AFTERWARD

In 1982 my family moved to Chicago from my native England. I was introduced to Grandmaster Chang in January 1983 as a shy 12 year old. He has been my teacher ever since.

I learnt both Ki Meditation and the Korean martial art of Hapkido from Master Chang in tandem; these two practices are intrinsically woven together within me. To discuss one without mention of the other would be as if I was holding part of me back. You will hear me, therefore, referring to Hapkido throughout this text. Physical techniques are but one aspect of Hapkido training; training in Hapkido involves understanding oneself, one's relationships with others and one's place within society. The challenges I have faced in both pursuits have mirrored each other and indeed my daily life.

This book intends to capture the words and teachings of Master Chang, but does not allege to do justice to his wisdom. If it can offer some hints, or lead the reader toward a deeper understanding of himself, then success has been achieved. I don't claim to possess the wisdom of Master Chang. All I hope for though is that he would read this book and recognise his loyal student.

Master Chang has been running 'Daybreak Ki Class' at his Chicago school since moving there in the early seventies. The class starts regularly at 5.30AM, so passing my driving exams at 16 was a prerequisite, especially for my mother who had been my chauffeur up to this point. As soon as I had my own drivers' license and access to my mum's car though, I immediately began the daily routine of daybreak Ki class.

Many were aghast when I mentioned attending a class so early in the morning. Being quite fond of sleep, I can see their point- but morning meditation has a wonderfully stimulating quality to it as energy naturally rises before midday. From a purely aesthetic point of view, there is also something quite magical about watching the world wake up around you.

In those early teenage years I can't say that I really understood what I was doing at Ki Class. I was there because my teacher had told me I should be; and I dutifully followed all the instructions he gave. That rationale was more than good enough for me.

At home I read any eastern philosophy book I could get my hands on. Unlike today, where even my local newsagent is selling a book on Karma, one had to seek out specialist bookstores to find anything half way decent. I soon got a reputation in my family for reading 'weird books'; it was their way of saying they were proud of the passion I seemed to be expressing for something, without really understanding what I was so passionate about. Speaking with my mother recently she talked of how her previously under-confident daughter started to blossom under the tutelage of Master Chang. I find it incredible how life can turn such a significant corner with one decision. Even to this day, how influential the choice to join Master Chang's school has been, astounds me.

Until I was twenty-four I continued training regularly with Master Chang. By this time I was leading morning classes, attending afternoon classes and, of course, diligently waking up each morning at 4.30am to come to Ki Class.

If I had had any choice in the matter I would never have left his school, or indeed America. A combination of bad legal advice, a limited amount of job experience and pure ignorance of the American immigration system resulted in a stream of problems. It started with me, a British subject, popping to Canada and being refused entry back into the States, and ended with me coming to the decision that I had to voluntarily deport myself.

Leaving America and my family and returning to England was a traumatic experience. I felt anger, panic and a huge sense of grief. Not knowing where to go, I moved in with my Grandma in Gainsborough, Lincolnshire. I had not seen her, my Aunt or cousins for about 11 years, but they opened their arms to me and welcomed me home.

Ki Meditation and Hapkido had been such an enormous part of my life that I felt a huge absence. I practiced daily on my Grandma's driveway, much to the fascination of her neighbours, and I continued reading my "weird books" and the pages of notes I had taken from Master Chang's many lectures. But the sense of loss I felt from leaving my teacher was tangible. After a few months I wrote him a letter. I can't even remember what it said, but I sent it next day delivery, and as soon as it arrived he called. The conversation was short, but went something like this.

MC: Tammy-ya

Me: Hello sir.

MC: You start to teach. Set up school. I will come to England. We have seminar. You tell me when.

Me: Yes, sir.

MC: Everything else okay?

Me: Yes Sir

MC: Good. You call me; tell me when you are ready.

ME: Yes, sir.

Click.

And so Chang's Hapkido Academy UK began. I taught both Ki and Hapkido in Lincolnshire from 1994 to 2001. Then I moved to London, where I have been teaching ever since. My teacher continues to travel to England 3-4 times per year, and I visit him in America as regularly as possible. I am humbled by the support and love he has shown me. I have always felt incredible loyalty to Master Chang, but for a long time I didn't fully understand why he would do this for me. Now that I have my own students I understand a little more.

WORKS CITED

Gershon, M. (1998). *The Second Brain.* HaperCollins Publishers.

Haslam , A. (2008, April 21). *How stereotypes can lead to success.* Retrieved from University of Exeter: http://www.exeter.ac.uk/news/archive/2008/april/title,1439,en.html

Lao Tsu. (n.d.). *Tao Te Ching* (September 1972 ed.). (G.-F. Feng, & J. English, Trans.) Vintage Books.

Medina, J. (2008, May). The Science of Thinking Smarter. *Harvard Business Review*, 51-54.

Oakley, R. (n.d.). How the Mind Hurts and Heals the Body. *American Psychologist, 59*(1).

Telles, S., & Naveen, K. (n.d.). Voluntary Breath Regulation in Yoga: It's Relevance and Physiological Effects. *Association for Applied Psychophysiology & Biofeedback, 36*(2), 70-73.